"A must-read for anyone interested i
as those interested in film in genera
informative study of the working director going through their creative paces."

— Brent Karl Clackson, producer: *Dead Like Me, The Highlander,
The Outer Limits*

"This is an absolutely indispensable guide to the real deal — what it's really like in the center of the maelstrom — the absolute giddy insanity, endless decisions, chasing the clock, working the politics, manic entity that *is* the world of the director. I've been running my game for decades and I *still* hide this book in my luggage, from country to county, and secretly review — sometimes just before I step back into the breach. Thank you, Charles!"

— David Winning, director of 13 features, 25 series, 100+ episodes for TV

"Making movies is Charles' life mission and in *The Working Film Director* he shows you how to accomplish that goal with passion and determination. If there's one thing I've learned in my 39 years in the film business, it's to remain human at all costs, and in this new edition Charles guides you through the necessary steps on how to accomplish that — by giving you the tools to cope with today's film industry politics while maintaining your dignity and living your life as a creative artist."

— Peter D. Marshall, filmmaker, educator; ActionCutPrint.com

"A Norwegian proverb states: 'Experience is the best teacher, but the tuition is high.' Charles Wilkinson has paid that tuition and now passes the lessons learned on to others for the mere price of this book. Success in our current film industry requires so much more than technique and technology. Somehow Charles is able to give a realistic, no-holds-barred view of today's marketplace and still leave the reader inspired and energized. The new chapters and revisions make this 2nd edition even more valuable and necessary for the emerging director than the original book."

— Richard Bellis, Emmy Award-winning composer, teacher,
author: *The Emerging Film Composer*

"This new edition of *The Working Film Director* is still the only book I've seen that talks about exactly what *is* and what *is not* the director's job. The new chapters provide powerful tools for navigating through the rapidly changing film world. Everyone who works on a film set needs to read this."

— Tobias Schliessler ASC, Director of Photography: *Battleship, Dreamgirls,
Friday Night Lights*

"The world of directing is always evolving. Wilkinson gives the reader invaluable new information to help them become a working director. I've now directed a number of episodes of *Army Wives* and I still find insight in his words."

— Brian McNamara, actor, director: *Seinfeld, NYPD Blue, Arachnophobia,
Army Wives*

"*The Working Film Director* not only gives you great advice as a future director, but insights into making the right choices for your career. It brings the reality of the film industry to life."

— Libby Blood, Associate Editor, *School Video News*

"If you're looking for a book that teaches you to analyze story, set up great shots, or work with amazing actors... this isn't it. *The Working Film Director* tells you the other stuff you need to know: how to navigate a location shoot, what to prepare for pre-production, how to work with DPs and visual effects artists. In other words, all the little details most people only gain from years of experience. Fortunately for you, Charles Wilkinson has just packed them into one book."

— Chad Gervich, writer/producer: *After Lately, Wipeout, Cupcake Wars*; author: *Small Screen, Big Picture: A Writer's Guide to the TV Business*

Second Edition

The *Working* Film
DIRECTOR

How to Arrive, Survive & *Thrive* in The Director's Chair

CHARLES WILKINSON

Published by Michael Wiese Productions
12400 Ventura Blvd. #1111
Studio City, CA 91604
tel. 818.379.8799
fax 818.986.3408
mw@mwp.com
www.mwp.com

Cover design: Johnny Ink www.johnnyink.com
Book design: Gina Mansfield Design
Copy editor: Matt Barber

Printed by McNaughton & Gunn, Inc., Saline, Michigan
Manufactured in the United States of America

Library of Congress Cataloging-in-Publication Data

Wilkinson, Charles, 1952 Mar. 2-
  The working film director : how to arrive, survive, and thrive in the direc-
tor's chair / Charles Wilkinson. -- 2nd ed.
    p. cm.
  ISBN 978-1-61593-132-3
  1. Motion pictures--Production and direction--Vocational guidance. 2.
Television--Production and direction--Vocational guidance. I. Title.
  PN1995.9.P7W55 2013
  791.4302'33023--dc23
                        2012027341

TABLE OF CONTENTS

ACKNOWLEDGEMENTS

∾

Many people contributed to the experiences this book is based on. Writers, actors, other directors, producers, distributors, critics, agents, publishers, crews, mentors, students, friends, foes, and family. In random order: Allen Epstein, Catherine Lough Hagquist, Linda Saint, Ken Gord, Jim Green, Jerry Wasserman, Melissa Gilbert, Don S. Williams, Tobias, Adrian Paul, John Juliani, Pierre Trudeau, Lenka Svab, Dave Hardon, Sgt. Don Hanson, Anemone Schliessler, Crawford Hawkins, Mark Bacino, David Hauka, Jennifer Clement, Bruce Weitz, Dolph Lundgren, Gordon Pinsent, Sharon McGowan, my brothers Lorne and Will. My parents Jack and Hazel.

Most of all: Nadya, Pablo, Fabio, and Tina.

How To Use This Book

Read it.

I read somewhere that the overwhelming majority of people never read beyond the "Quick Start Guide" that comes with their new phone. I also read that most people never use 90% of the features their phone is capable of. Think there may be a relationship between these two things?

The best way to use this book is to read it through, bookmarking, highlighting ideas you want to come back to, making notes.

But maybe you're starting prep on a studio blockbuster in the morning and the biggest set you've ever been on had five people. Or maybe you're sitting behind a difficult editor thinking murderous thoughts. Or maybe you're "between jobs," standing in a bookstore wondering if this is worth the cover price.

You want the info you need *now*. So here's your quick-start guide:

— **Beginners.** Not sure if this is the job for you? Chapter 1.

— **Beginners not wanting to waste money on film school.** Chapter 2.

— **Filmmakers in a hurry to break in.** "The Secret." (Pg. 9)

— **Film students.** "Making the Most Of Film School." (Pg. 17)

— **First-film filmmakers.** Chapter 3.

— **Stalled, crashed, burned filmmakers.** Chapter 3.

— **Festival submitters.** Chapter 4.

— **Selling that film?** Chapter 5.

— **Moving?** Find where the work is in Chapter 6.

— **Just offered a job?** Before you call back, read Chapter 7.

— **Prep problems?** You'll likely find answers in Chapter 8.

— **On-set issues?** Take a stroll through Chapter 9.

— **Quitting?** It may not be all that bad. Read Chapter 10.

— **Editors.** Struggling with that director? Get them to read Chapter 11.

— **Sound designing & mixing?** What are all those knobs for? See Chapter 11.

— **That's a Wrap!** Finished? Not until you read Chapter 12.

FOREWORD
TO THE 2ND EDITION

This is the best time ever to become a director!

In spite of all the recent developments that might suggest the working director has become something of an endangered species, in spite of all the dark clouds, there are some incredibly bright rays of sunshine. The situation on the ground has changed tremendously since the 1st Edition of *The Working Film Director* was published. This new edition addresses changes like:

- How to get started from the new ground zero.
- Film school or not, how to choose one and what to demand.
- The first film — low-budget, micro-budget, 5D, or the guaranteed route.
- The first film festivals — which ones, how to get in, how to maximize the returns.
- Selling that first film — count your fingers.
- How to convert the first film into a career.
- The career stall or crash — what to do when the phone stops ringing.

In addition, the rest of the content has been updated to fit the current, and likely future, rules. There are sections on:

- Where to locate.
- Getting hired.
- Maximizing pre-production.
- On-set protocol.
- Earning respect on set.
- Avoiding conflict in post-production.
- Finishing well.
- Getting the next job.

For new readers of the book, I believe you'll find a really useful set of guidelines, rules, and tips for how to successfully enter and grow in this most wonderful career. For the returning reader familiar with the previous edition, beside a thorough update of all material, I think you'll especially find the entirely new first third of the book vitally important reading as you deal with all the new twists on your journey to arrive, thrive, and survive in that director's chair.

Let's talk about the game change that's been unfolding.

The five years that have passed since the original publication of *The Working Film Director* have seen dramatic changes in the world of the film and television director. Numerous factors have contributed; the polarization of the feature market between blockbusters and low-budget first films, the rise of the 500-channel universe, the resulting fall of advertising revenue-supported network programming, the overcrowding and consequent decline of the TV syndication market, the rise of Netflix and other video-on-demand services, the consequent death of home video rental, and most troubling — the wildfire of unpaid, illegal Internet downloading. To the working director, these developments pose significant challenges.

These are not the only, nor even the most serious, challenges within the film industry. The industry has been impacted by a deteriorating world security situation since 9/11. International work permits have become more difficult to get. Trade protectionism, a factor previously uncommon in international filmmaking, has grown. And the worldwide economic crisis sparked by the U.S. sub-prime mortgage collapse continues to severely restrict money supply — especially to speculative ventures like film production. All of these factors have served to limit the working director's supply of career opportunities.

On the demand side — the number of new directors competing for work is skyrocketing. Steadily improving quality of film school education provided by older, qualified filmmakers migrating into more reliable work at the ever-growing number of film schools is resulting in unheard of numbers of trained, aggressive, would-be working directors entering the marketplace. In short, we seem to have a situation for the working director that could be described as a "perfect storm."

That's pretty discouraging. Now here comes the good part:

Never before in human history have we had the unfettered, unregulated ability to communicate our personal thoughts and beliefs to such vast numbers of fellow human beings across almost all international boundaries. Since the invention of mass media, the high cost of production has concentrated control in relatively few hands. Mass communication was possible — but who got to communicate? There have always been filters between those doing the communicating and those watching and listening — corporate-run studios, networks, theater chains. They got to decide. Yes, there have always been people and organizations that strived to produce intelligent, important, truthful and innovative films and television — programs that entertained, informed, inspired, uplifted. Just not a whole lot of them.

[Tobias photo]

That's about to change.

Today, the gatekeepers — the filters between those doing the communicating and those watching and listening — are being swept away. Consider: using simple, readily available tools, anyone can make a movie about their cat using the toilet and have it watched — without any type of effective middleman being involved — by hundreds of millions of people.

The Iliad, The Odyssey, Citizen Kane, a cat using a toilet. Wow.

But wait. If the cat-on-the-toilet epic is possible — *what isn't?*

That's the amazing thing. *Anything* is now possible.

Way back in 1990 or so, director/genius Francis Ford Coppola famously said:

"One day some little fat girl in Ohio is going to be the new Mozart."

That day is here. I visit a lot of film festivals. I see this happening all around me. I watched a remarkable dramatic feature at a festival the other day, a film with good production values, with actors, great locations, music, action, and a really fascinating message. The film cost under $10,000 and was shot by a crew of three. The film is being seen in theaters across America. It's been purchased for TV broadcast.

At this writing I am currently touring the festival circuit with a documentary feature I directed about a subject I care passionately about, a story I felt the mainstream was missing. I didn't ask anyone's permission. I didn't pitch anyone. I didn't beg anyone's agent. I believed in an idea, I went out and made the film for bus fare and donuts. *Peace Out* is playing around the world, generating intelligent discussion, changing minds.

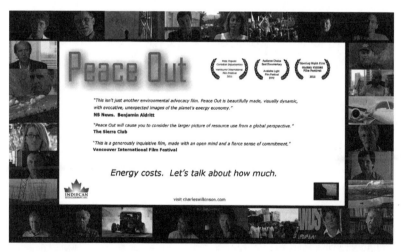

[Charles Wilkinson photo]

Am I saying that Hollywood is burning? Not at all. But Hollywood is *noticing*. Why? Gone are the days when we have to pay to see how empty the latest "blockbuster" is. One friend goes, texts the rest of us and we stay away and click on a link to this amazing Vimeo clip about — you name it. Like our cat/toilet video, ideas suddenly have the potential to "go viral." Stop for a minute and think how remarkable that is. Unmediated communication from the girl in Ohio, direct to everyone.

This is as close to global telepathy as we've seen.

And yes, "Hollywood," which is to say the corporate entertainment industry, is listening. Take a look at the fresh crop of releases — there are more first-time directors than ever, more big-budget films with social media stars replacing established actors. And now every mainstream film works the Internet and social media sites. The lessons of *The Blair Witch Project* have revolutionized, and to a very real degree democratized, movie advertising. Studios are leaping onto the Twitter bandwagon, seeking that elusive "viral" effect. Sometimes it works. *The Hunger Games* saturated social media and opened huge. Sometimes not. All the social media in the world couldn't save *John Carter*.

So the process is becoming democratized. So? Is the audience being *captured* by the cat on the toilet? Of course not. We all click on the links, we experience the giddy freedom of un-censored content. But… the cat pretty much just sits there. It would be great if it were in some way *endearing*, if it had some kind of goal, if it had to overcome some kind of really insurmountable obstacles so we could root for it. Some better camera and sound work would help. Some music, maybe a bit of CGI to get the cat to speak. We'd probably need someone to coordinate all that stuff. We could call them a… See where this is heading?

The world *loves* good movies. Good movies need good directors. The talented and committed rise to the top. Visit the film festivals, look at what's winning. Look at what's making it into the theaters and onto TV. Pictures are being made that are pushing back the boundaries of the craft, the boundaries of human experience. The industry is in a near chaotic state, trying to figure out how to ride this tiger of unprecedented audience participation.

Here's a certainty: *someone* is going to direct the new films and television. No one knows who. Let me amend that. Only two of us know who it's going to be. I know it's going to be you.

It's not going to be easy. You're going to have to work incredibly hard, clear extraordinary hurdles, have a lot of luck. The purpose of this book is to point you at some of the tools you're going to need to get there. But getting there is do-able. More do-able today than ever before.

Consider this: It has become relatively common to read that a young filmmaker who's written a powerful screenplay or has self-produced a

5D feature has received studio financing for a mainstream project. This is someone without connections, no uncles at Universal, someone who hasn't schmoozed the parties, someone who hasn't even got an agent. Yet this filmmaker has cleared an enormous hurdle on the way to becoming a working director. How did she do it? This is what the first part of *The Working Film Director* is about.

A note on gender language. "He/she" is awkward. "They" is often worse. Our business has made tremendous gains in the area of gender equality. Women and men are largely interchangeable and receive equal pay. So I will arbitrarily refer to a cinematographer for example as "her" or "him" for the sake of flow without meaning to imply that DPs are all female or all male.

To continue with our hypothetical first-timer, once she signs with the studio her status changes radically. Our director must go from working alone in a basement to interacting with an enormous jumbo jet-like machine peopled by executives, producers, actors, professional crew, publicists, agents, and critics. Whether this director spent years at film school and as an apprentice on professional sets like Steven Spielberg, or was self-taught like Robert Rodriguez, she must now perform a series of complex procedures and avoid a series of complex pitfalls.

Learning to recognize and work the controls of that jumbo jet is what the second part of *The Working Film Director* is about.

Let me use a video game analogy to describe what this book is really trying to be. People who spend time with video games know that there are online sites and books that provide tips, clues, and assists to the gamer. Things like, "*at the end of the hall, behind the garbage can there's a small golden key — pick it up.*" You *might* find the key without the tip. You might not. The tip moves you toward your goal much quicker — which is something most of us would value. There are a lot of tips in this book — because there's a lot a working director needs to know.

While some things in our industry have transformed, many others have not. The job interview, working with writers, location planning and shot making, directing the crew, actors, post-production discipline — all of these crafts may evolve cosmetically, but they remain fundamentally unchanged. These too are the things that *The Working Film Director* is about.

A programming director friend of mine at a medium-sized international film festival recently challenged me to guess how many independent feature film submissions they had received from just one small country this year. In light of the global economic woes, I guessed a dozen. Her answer — more than 500. Out of which she had difficulty selecting a half-dozen good films. *Something* makes those half-dozen films stand apart from the 494 others. This is the director's *craft*.

Yes, the reality on the ground for the working director is shifting dramatically over a very short timeframe. But directors everywhere continue to practice a complex craft — in some traditional ways, and in many new, innovative ways. Hopefully, you will find tools in the following pages that help you to do both, as you become and remain — a working director.

Before we dive in, let's define some terms.

For the sake of this discussion, a **working director** is someone who gets paid to direct mainstream film and television.

Mainstream film and television is defined here as either dramatic or documentary fare that is programmed at film festivals, screened in commercial theaters, and broadcast on commercial TV. YouTube content or sponsored programming falls outside of this category.

Back in the 1950s, when TV really took off the word was that movies were dead — who'd come out and pay to watch when they could stay home and watch for free? Then in the '80s the blockbusters were going to kill smaller, idea-oriented films. Today we're told that the Internet is putting the final nails in film and television's coffin. *All wrong.* We love good movies. Good movies take a tremendous amount of skill to make. The people who take the time to acquire those skills are going to direct those good movies. American philosopher Henry David Thoreau once said:

"If you have built castles in the air, your work need not be lost; that is where they should be. Now put foundations under them."

Let's pour some concrete together.

Charles Wilkinson
Pacific North Coast, 2012

INTRODUCTION

"You directors, the second you turn in a picture that doesn't work, it's 'art' this and 'integrity' that. I hire and fire you bums like extras."
— My first job interview

This book is not about where to put the camera.

It's not about the great masters of the cinema.

This book is about one thing: getting paid to direct film and television.

More to the point, this book is about how to make that happen. It's about how to keep it happening, and how to jump-start it when it falters. It's not that where you put the camera is unimportant or that the masters aren't worthy of study. It is and they are. *The Working Film Director* is going to talk about a different aspect of your craft.

A tiny percentage of film directors are established directors — those highly paid professionals who have relatively free choice over what they direct. At the other end of the spectrum there are the teeming multitudes of unpaid or "prosumer" directors — those who work without pay and show their work for free over the Internet. The established director's career goal is to stay on top. The unpaid director's career goal is to become established. In between these two groups are the working directors.

The vast majority of movies, TV films, episodes, and documentaries are directed by us — the working directors. Who are we?

When a movie performs well — either by winning major awards or making significant money, or both — two paths open up. In the case of runaway success the director tends to be given a real shot at becoming an established director. That's 1% of the time. The other 99% of the time, when a show doesn't bomb but enjoys less than runaway success, the director often receives offers to direct more modest fare — *as a working director*. A sports analogy might be that we're the farm team, which is defined by Wikipedia as:

Farm Team: a team or club whose role is to provide experience and train-ing for young players, with an agreement that any successful players can move on to a higher level at a given point.

The agreement regarding moving up is pretty simple — *make something that experiences runaway success.*

But, until that time, we have the infinite joy of directing the majority of film and television. That's us — the working directors. We get paid. This is key — it allows us to quit our day jobs and spend all our time getting better. We take material that is often flawed and perform heroics translat-ing the amazing idea in the writer's head into an amazing experience in the audience's head such that we move on up to the majors — or not. The great success of achieving "mere" working director status is that life is pretty awesome on the farm team too.

Very few established directors achieve that status without paying their due down in our ranks. And I've never met a serious un-paid director who wouldn't sacrifice a great deal to achieve the success of a mere working director.

For every director — the un-paid and the established ones included — sometimes a show turns out well, sometimes not. And even when a movie turns a profit and garners good reviews, you'd think career advancement would be more or less guaranteed. But it's not. The truth is, short of a $100-million-dollar weekend or an Academy Award, no matter how our shows turn out the director is up against serious competition for *every* directing job. And there are things we all do or neglect to do every day that affect our chances of being hired.

There are many terrific books on the world of the established director. There are also several fine books on the world of the un-paid director. At present there is very little by way of published discussion on the world of the successful working director.

Why is that important? Because our ground rules are different. The estab-lished director has, within the context of the film, a power so absolute it approaches that of ancient kings. The working director, by contrast, is an *employee.* In the working director's world, the *producer* has the power of kings. Including the power to hire you. Or not. That makes a world of difference.

For example: In both the established director's world and the un-paid director's world the lead actors are cast (which is to say *hired*) by you, the director. Their allegiance is to you. In the working director's world the lead actors are most often cast by the producer. They are frequently more important to the financing than you are. Their allegiance is to their role or the producer or their public. But not necessarily to you. This book is about acquiring techniques for finding your place in this mix and using those tools to do the good work you must do.

Another example: As an established director, or even the un-paid director, you often have wide powers over the script. You can make changes as you deem necessary. As a working director it's not at all uncommon for producers to discourage the changing of a single *word*. This book is about acquiring techniques for getting the script changes you need to tell the story without risking unnecessary conflict.

The Working Film Director follows a linear format, leading from a discussion of how to move from un-paid status up to that all-important first phone call, on through prep, production and post, right up to getting your next and better job. Here's how I'm defining "better job":

Your phone rings. A script arrives at your door. A good one. A check arrives by courier. A big one. A driver picks you up in a car. A new smelling one. These people in this office are nice to you. Really nice. You chair meetings. Interesting, harmonious, creative meetings. Everyone listens to you. A crew of capable workers assembles. They jump at your invitation to collaborate. A group of talented actors appears before your eyes. They accept you into their sandbox. You say the magic word, "*Action.*" Everything springs to life. Every fiber of your creative energy flows into the creation of a stream of images and sounds that, when placed in front of millions of viewers, provokes thought, laughter, tears, inspiration. The critics rave. Flowers arrive at your door. You've just made your mark on history.

[With DP Michael Slovis on *Harvest*. Tina Schliessler photo]

This is the best job in the world. Bar none. But is there a catch? Yes, thousands of them. Some people attain the status of rising working director only to find a different reality, one that goes like this:

Your phone rings. A script arrives at your door. It "needs work." The people in the office are civil. To your face. You attend meetings. Fractious, inconclusive, angry meetings. People listen to you. Then they do it the way they feel like doing it. A crew of workers assembles grudgingly. A group of yesterday's actors appears before your eyes. One or more won't come out of their trailer. You say the magic word, "*Action*." Everything limps to life. Every fiber of your creative energy (except those fibers devoted to watching your back) flows into the creation of a stream of at best adequate images and sounds that, when placed in front of millions of viewers provokes a "mixed response." The critics pan it. No flowers, no friends, no history. Just rumors that there were "problems" on set. Your phone goes dead.

It gets that bad and worse. Everything is so volatile. Make a few key mistakes and see how fast Scenario A becomes Scenario B. Make some good catches, have a few heart to hearts with the right people, connect with, even *galvanize* the unit, and B becomes A.

We work in a pressure cooker. Even a small unit costs someone a huge amount of money to run every day, every hour. Even micro-budget shows cost money that's needed for rent. Money that everyone on set knows *your* work had better convince an audience to part with. We have weather pressure, time pressure, creative pressure, interpersonal pressure, tribal pressure, *tire* pressure for God's sake (a blown tire can cost an hour, a day, a human life). We work under the pressure of insanely long hours. Frequently in demanding, uncomfortable places. We suffer the pressure of days, weeks, months living, eating, working, like sardines in a can, with large groups of strangers. And when it's finally over, we often suffer the gnawing anxiety a telephone creates by simply not ringing.

Best job in the world when things go right. When they don't, a not so great job. Established director or emerging hopeful, the script arrives at your door and you take your chances. Luck of the draw.

Or is it?

If you're going to take credit for how well Scenario A works out, doesn't that mean you kind of have to accept at least some of the blame for how badly Scenario B unfolds?

Yes.

Is there anything you can do to prevent Scenario B from happening again?

Yes.

Will you find answers in these pages?

Yes.

Some you'll already know. Many are self-evident. Some you won't agree with. And some are just real hard to practice. But hopefully the ideas you find here will get you focusing on aspects of your craft you've never considered before.

Some of what I have to say is aimed at emerging directors. And I'll note that where appropriate. Some of what I have to say is aimed respectfully at the established professionals beginning to look over their shoulders. But the bulk of what follows is meant for the working director. Whether it's your first show or your hundredth. Because until you achieve established director status, the rules are the rules.

But you say, *my talent is all I need. As long as I do good work, none of this other stuff matters.*

Experience suggests otherwise.

"Established Director" status mostly doesn't last. When the Oscar-winning, blockbuster-delivering directors strike out a few times, they're often back to being employees in the working director realm. Scan the box office charts from just five years ago. Search the directors of those films on IMDb.com. See for yourself.

The fact is that directors who continue to work tend to be advice takers. We seek out every scrap of knowledge on how to ply the craft to get the absolute maximum out of our people and avoid the destructive and time-wasting landmines our projects are seeded with.

Film is an intensely social medium. Directors are by definition "people people." The cliché of the brooding loner who appears on set, does the magic silently and departs in mystery is generally a myth. Most directors talk a lot. They have to. There are so many choices. Brown hat or black? Mercedes or BMW? 85mm or 50mm? Sadder or happier? Bigger or smaller? Chocolate or vanilla? Literally *thousands* of questions a day. Certainly there are directors who delegate many of these choices. The actors will direct themselves if you don't. The cinematographer can come up with a workable shot. The teamster can decide whether Thelma and Louise drive a classic T-Bird or the rusty Honda Civic he wants to rent to the production. Somebody always says. Somebody always chooses. Thousands of choices a day. And each one of those choices has the potential to come back to slam you.

And if you say, "All I have to do is do good work and nothing else matters," how exactly is good work measured?

Yes, a multimillion-dollar opening weekend is a no-brainer. But frequently the success of our shows is difficult to measure. What if you've just directed Episode 6 of this season's 22 episodes of *I Just Want My Pants*

Back? How do you measure that? Weekly ratings don't really measure you. It's not like they advertised the episode as being *un film de* you. Similarly, network executives and producers don't always credit the directors for the good ratings of their TV movies or mini-series. They speak instead of how the concept scored. Or the cast or the line-up. The only time TV is anything close to a director's medium is for those few brief moments on Emmy night. What about theatrical features? The industry leaders, to their credit, acknowledge that many factors create a success or failure at the box office. Cast, timing, script, promotion, what else is running. So the director of an unsuccessful theatrical is often given a second or third chance. Often, but not always. If not upon success then what is that decision to hire and re-hire you based on?

That is precisely what *The Working Film Director* is about. Getting work, doing work, getting more work.

Because to a director, not working is a slow death. You must work. Forget the money. (Sure, you also must eat, but if that was what it was about you'd have gone to dentistry school.) Forget whatever prestige might come with the job. You direct because you love to tell stories. You live for the look in your audience's eyes when your voice drops to a hushed whisper and you say, "*...She crept through the dank and glistening tunnel, an ominous breathing all about her, when suddenly... BOOM!!!*" And they jump, scream, laugh, and forget for a moment their mean science teacher or their overdue car payment or what the doctor said this afternoon.

That moment is something that exists between you and your audience. That more than anything else is the paycheck you receive for the work you do. But to get to that moment, to be able to repeat that moment with any regularity, you have to thread your way through some very complex mazes. You have to get the job. You have to do the job well. You have to make the friends who will hire you to do the job again.

This is what *The Working Film Director* is going to talk about.

Who am I to talk, you ask?

If there were an award category for *Dumbest Mistake on a Film or Television Show* I'd have a case full of golden statues. I've passed on major projects because I thought the shooting location was wrong. I've abandoned highly paid work in Paris to help with a sound mix on a previous, troubled film. I've put myself between screaming executives and decent crew members. I've allowed my own hurt feelings and wounded pride to goad me into unprofessional conduct. I've challenged corrupt film distributors who had numerous other shows they would otherwise have hired me for. I've told network executives poised to hire me that what I really wanted to do was features (*seriously! I actually did this!*). I've spent years asking the wrong people for the right things on and off set. I've more or less lived to tell the tale. In short, I'm a fairly typical working director.

My first "job" in the entertainment business was at the age of three. I had an imaginary radio show. I'd sing myself to sleep for hours every night. By the time I was six my big brother and I actually were regular singers on a popular radio show. We graduated to TV as series regulars on a popular variety show, recorded, toured. All before I was fourteen.

So I pretty much grew up chasing that moment. The moment the audience forgets everything and is just with you. I learned to love that. I love the feeling of aligning all the particles in the room. That's the breath of life.

[Author at age eleven with bad hat and guitar. Ed Kidd photo]

I went to film school. Before graduation I directed a documentary that won a few awards. I was hired by a small studio to direct another documentary far away from any supervision. I made the documentary — and secretly shot an impromptu feature at the same time with the same crew and the same budget. The documentary made a profit. The feature got a small theatrical release, scored (entirely justifiably) "mixed" reviews, and (surprisingly) my phone started ringing.

Since then I've directed four theatrically released features. All of them made money and now pop up regularly on late night TV opposite the infomercials. I've directed a number of well-received TV movies for the major networks, numerous episodic shows and documentaries. I've written screenplays that others have directed. I've said no to projects that felt wrong. I've weathered periods of unemployment and, equally challenging, periods of prosperity. This business introduced me to the most wonderful woman on Earth, who is also my best friend, we have a terrific family together. And together we've made a lot of pretty insane home movies on camping road trips to Mexico. More recently I've been lucky to have been able to transition from the dramas of "guys with guns and beautiful girls at risk" to the documentary cinema of ideas.

Through it all my phone has kept ringing.

Not because I've won an Oscar (probably never will). Not because I have Emmys (even less likely). Not because I'm a pushover to work with (ask anyone…).

The audience keeps us working directors busy for a list of reasons so long it would fill a book.

Here it is.

[With Dennis Weaver on ABC's *Harvest*. Myrl Coulter photo]

chapter one

TOUGH LOVE

S o far this has been pretty upbeat, I'd say. I'm afraid we're going to go dark for a bit. I don't like being negative, but sometimes tough love is the best kind. I apologize in advance and promise we'll get back into positive territory as soon as humanly possible.

Ready?

"I really want to direct."

Common phrase. You've heard it from rock stars, world leaders, at least one of the Popes, and that girl who works at Starbucks. Many spend a decade or more and thousands of dollars trying. And while some actually end up with the job, most don't. Urban legends about making it because of who one knows or what parties one goes to are common and, in some rare cases, true. But generally, those who end up directing do so because they have aptitude for the job and aptitude for hard work. Can this be measured? Happily, yes. By the time we get to the end of this chapter you're going to have a few tools that will help you decide. The first question is pretty straightforward:

DO YOU HAVE APTITUDE?

Here's an example of what I mean; next time you're in a casual social setting, eating or drinking with family or friends, quietly take ten minutes to select and organize the one single event you'd describe as the most interesting thing that's ever happened to you. Then find a lull in the conversation and tell your story — in five minutes or less. Note the reaction.

If people say things like: "Wow, that was the most interesting story I've ever heard" or "That was just so touching, so inspiring" or "I've never laughed so hard in my entire life," I'd say there's a very high probability you have aptitude.

Introverts do occasionally succeed in the job. Both Clint Eastwood and Woody Allen are said to be introverts. Clint established his brand as an actor first, however, and Woody has always done spectacular stand-up. And, interestingly, both have always loved performing publicly as musicians.

Aptitude For Hard Work?

Pick a successful director, research their early life. The majority started making films very young. How about you? Many of you have been making videos since childhood. Some of you have already racked up some pretty impressive festival wins. Again, if this is you — terrific!

But what if it isn't you? What if you're an awkward introvert with no real proven background in filmmaking. Are you doomed? Let's step outside the box some.

Chances are most of us won't become Formula One drivers. We may have a driver's license, a car, maybe we even like driving fast. But the amount of native ability, commitment, obsession, and luck it takes to actually race in Formula One is so extreme that maybe 1 in 100,000 who try will ever make it.

Did you think that directing film and television would be any easier?

WHY AM I BEING SO NEGATIVE?

Don't get me wrong. *I'm on your side here.* I find myself in a remarkable position. I've been inexplicably blessed to have been a working director for three decades. I've also had the great good fortune to have been able to attempt to teach often wonderful young women and men while continuing to write and direct. And I'm now at a point where I don't much worry about offending studio, network, industry, or academic people. I can say what I believe to be true.

So here's the thing: I feel just terrible when I meet a former classmate from my film school days or a student of mine years later and see that *failure* look in their downcast eyes. These are intelligent young men and women who could be making a real difference in finance or law or construction or healthcare or government. Instead they've spent the last decade or more working service jobs, hustling short films that play in half-full rep houses.

What if you're really not cut out for this? Imagine the reaction you're going to get ten years from now from everyone you told about your dream to direct. Was that an eye roll you just got from the guy who used to look up to you in high school? I don't mean your lack of money, houses, cars, status, or kids. I'm talking about your self-respect based on a life lived deliberately and well. *That's* what I'm hoping for you. If it turns out you beat the odds — great. But if you think deeply and decide right now that you actually really enjoy welding — weld!

The coolest, happiest, most creative and satisfied people I know are not directors. Think about that for a minute. What's your goal in life? Most people, once they drill down beneath all the media noise and cliché, would say things like: I want to pull my weight, do something worthwhile and meaningful, find love, be satisfied, fulfilled, and so on. Let me say it again:

The coolest, happiest, most creative and satisfied people I know are <u>not</u> directors.

But you're not buying this love, peace, and chicken grease stuff, right? You *have* to direct. You <u>feel</u> it. You'll beat the odds, blaze your own trail. Great! As I say, that's what we're here for. But it's still good to know what you're getting into. Let's talk about that for a while. It may be time well spent.

The small amount I've learned over a long career of directing film and television tells me the first and most important thing we need to talk about here is....

Why Do You Even Want To Direct?

Why are you drawn to this? I meet an awful lot of people who express a desire to be a director. I meet a far smaller number of people who truly *want to direct*. See the difference? The reasons I hear for why someone wants the job generally boil down to these few:

1. Cliché
2. Money
3. Altruism
4. Aptitude

1. Cliché: "*Directors are never in short supply of girlfriends.*" — Bob Fosse

Our culture confers upon the film director a god-like status. From the outside looking in it appears that you're the boss. You command huge crews, enormous sums of money, cinema idols. You hang out with presidents and rock stars. You travel to space, to the bottom of the ocean. What's not to like about that?

Of the students I work with, on average 85% say they want to be directors. It's pretty much a knee-jerk reaction. Many of them have even picked a production company name and have printed up business cards. I'm afraid much of that motivation comes from the culture. I've seen it at work. My parents used to worry about me — I was a really late bloomer (a bum, basically). They had to endure their friend's bragging about little Dougie becoming a doctor and little Gwenny designing a bridge. When I finally started working, the tables so turned. For my mom to say, "Our Charlie had a movie on ABC last night that played in twenty million homes across America…." that gave her a lot of pleasure. But to their great credit my folks never pushed me. They always displayed a very healthy scepticism about the job — as in "When are you going to get a real one?" So I'm going to call out all you moms and dads here.

Parents, encouraging your kids is one thing. I get that you worry your kids will never put down the game console, move out of the basement, and take an interest in something — anything. My parents worried about me. I worried about my kids. But I never pushed them to follow in my footsteps. Know why? It's hard enough to beat the odds and make it as a director. The last thing kids need is that extra pressure from *your* expectations. No one makes it in this business without being seriously *driven.* And if your kids discover they're driven, your lack of pushing won't amount to much of an obstacle.

My kids played with video cameras growing up. They had fun. Like I used to have fun building and racing slot cars when I was their age. I'm sure at some point they may have dreamed of entering the business — they certainly got to raid enough amazing craft service tables on the shows I did. But they weren't *consumed* with desire, so I didn't push them. Today they're happy in their chosen crafts and I couldn't be more proud of them.

What's wrong with chasing a dream if it makes them happy? Unfortunately, very often it makes them really *unhappy*. Imagine meeting an old friend from high school ten years later who's poised to jump off a bridge lamenting, "Yeah, I gave becoming a realtor my best shot. I just wasn't good enough."

Directing is a job.

It's also a calling. As is medicine, the law, construction, public relations. And like these other callings, directing takes its own certain skill set, a set of qualities, and <u>attributes</u>. I meet parents pushing their kids to become directors. I'll often ask them why they don't encourage them to become doctors, lawyers, engineers. They'll usually laugh at the thought of their kid putting forth this much discipline, commitment, and sheer *drive*. Guess what, Mom, Dad — becoming a competent director is every bit as hard — maybe harder. Ignore the clichés. They're a mirage.

[Marg Helgenberger with some of my students on the *CSI* set. Charles Wilkinson photo]

2. **Money**: "*Directors work ten times harder than anyone else. Get paid a quarter.*" — William H. Macy

Getting into this for the pay is like saying you want to go into politics because the president of the U.S. makes $400,000 a year. Few honest politicians make much money. Neither do most directors. For all but the top tier, someone with the skills to direct could make more in any other profession. Seriously. No one becomes a director to get rich. It happens occasionally, sure. But most times you read the numbers on a big check, think, "Wow, that's kind of cool," then go back to work. And after your next year of unemployment it's all gone.

3. **Altruism**: "*If you want to send a message use Western Union.*" — Sam Goldwyn

That's pretty cynical. After all, movies like *American Beauty* and *Cabaret* do get made and they do change our lives for the better. Wanting to make our world better is a noble goal. But I don't often see it sustaining one in the director's chair. The directors who tend to make it are storytellers first and last. Their "messages" are what all decent and intelligent people think about — the conflict between good and evil, and how good just tends to work out better.

My experience with people who try to become directors of "meaningful" films is that they tend to end up outside the mainstream, making special audience films about the spiritual healing power of crystals, or how pollution is bad. Not that there's anything wrong with that. But our focus here is mainstream fare that people pay to see. I'm not saying Sam Goldwyn was right. We live to make a difference with our work. But that's got to be the verdict — not the occupation.

4. **Aptitude**: "*All directors are storytellers. That's what I love.*" — Spike Lee

This is the good one. By aptitude I mean a lot of different things. There's an acquired skill set, yes. Like medicine, it's a really complex field and there's a ton to learn if you want to be any good at it. But there are also attitudes and innate qualities that a director must possess.

The test I advised you to take at the beginning of the chapter is a pretty reliable measure of aptitude. A terrific example of this in the cinema is Quentin Tarantino's "Like a Virgin" monologue near the beginning of *Reservoir Dogs*. Tarantino's character, Mr. Brown — by no means the heavyweight at the table — captures the attention and even admiration of all these very tough customers with a successful piece of storytelling. How? He selects a subject his audience is deeply interested in (promiscuous sex), he employs a fresh and unusual approach to his material, and he uses a good deal of profanity and outrageous but clever humor. Mr. Brown is not what you'd call a nice guy. He isn't someone you'd want your sister dating. He'd never be cast as a romantic lead or a wise elder. He's just a *really* good storyteller. So, are all working directors gregarious, capable public speakers, great joke tellers, like Mr. Brown? Probably not. I just personally rarely meet one who isn't.

Yes, Quentin Tarantino and Sam Mendes and the Coen Brothers have serious messages. But their films are *entertaining* to watch. Otherwise people wouldn't watch them. Why is it some people who claim to want to be directors find the notion of becoming an entertainer so unappealing? A director is a *storyteller*. A storyteller who knows a wonderful story. A storyteller who intuits the heart of the listener, feels how they feel, and learns to shape that feeling. Is this you? If not, can these things be taught? I believe so, but I'm not completely certain — having not yet completely learned them myself in spite of decades of effort. I honestly can't tell you it's possible to learn what Francis Ford Coppola knows. But my experience down here with the working directors has shown me that there are certain tell-tale signs.

TAKE THE PEPSI CHALLENGE

- Do strangers celebrate your work?
- Have your student films been chosen again and again at film festivals in cities other than your own?
- Do your YouTube videos have thousands, even hundreds of thousands, of hits?
- When you speak in public, does everyone shut up, pay attention, then cheer?

∾ Are you good at self-promotion, shamelessly pushing yourself forward to the front of the line?

∾ Are you a natural leader — do people happily follow the clear instructions you give?

∾ Do you have something important to say, something strangers find fascinating?

∾ Do you cope well with highly negative criticism, utter rejection, and abject failure?

∾ Are you OK with extended bouts of poverty?

∾ Are you prepared to gamble away the next decade or two?

If you answer yes to most of these questions, then you're in the right place, reading the right book. If you look that list over and honestly realize you're answering "no" more often than "yes" — *run away*. If you haven't bent the pages of this book back too badly you might even get a refund (no promises). But don't sweat it. Find that <u>one</u> thing you're destined to be amazing at — the thing that will make your life the wonderful journey each human life deserves to be.

For those who choose to stay, it's time to get positive again. Let's go to work.

[Crew hard at work filming an action scene on *The Legend of the Ruby Silver*. Charles Wilkinson photo]

chapter two

THE FIRST BEST STEPS

Whats the straightest line between where you're sitting right this minute, and getting a real shot at becoming an established director?

As I write this, there's a first-time director in L.A. directing a $200-million action film. The buzz is that the director is an overnight discovery — he's only directed one short film and a national commercial. That's the buzz. The reality is that he's been making award-winning short films for years, he's directed a ton of commercials, he's connected like you wouldn't believe, and he's been pushing the right buttons hard for years to make a feature film. It sort of seems like the old "Catch-22" again. You can't get in unless you're already in, and that seems like it takes a decade at least.

There is, however, one way that first-timers can short-circuit the process and fast-track into the mainstream.

THE SECRET

There is a secret passageway leading from the room you are sitting in now, directly to the director's chair on a mainstream Hollywood motion picture. It is 100% foolproof. It is a secret so powerful that it rates its own page to exist on. Take a breath, then turn the page.

Get your hands on a great script.

That's it.

OK, I didn't say there wasn't going to be stuff you have to do *after* you've got that script. There is. In order:

Craft an excellent log line.

Find out who rep'd the writers on a half dozen successful films in your genre.

Contact the agents. One will bite. If not, return to previous page.

This is the plain, unvarnished truth.

I was talking with a friend of mine the other day who works near the top of the food chain in Hollywood. I asked him what the most common way in was for new directors. His answer ran something like: "At least twice a month I'll see a green-lit project by a first-time director cross my desk. In every case the project is script-driven."

I asked him about the current buzz surrounding the self-financed 5D features — shows where a young filmmaker will go out with a small group of like-minded friends and simply shoot a micro-budget feature, then try the festival circuit or put it up on YouTube to see the response. His response was that the buzz around this approach is building, but the great script method is the one that works most often.

I asked him: What about the guys who scrape together a million or so to shoot their low-budget calling card? His reaction: A million-dollar show without a terrific script is no more likely to launch its director than a 5D picture.

Next I called a friend who programs for a major film festival. His reaction was eye-opening as well. "I see many hundreds of independent films submitted every year. Most films today have adequate production values. My audiences watch low production value films like *Waste Land* and *Exit Through The Gift Shop*. They don't care if you used a 5D or a Panaflex. It's the power of the subject and the intelligence of the story that puts bums in seats. And 99% of the independent dramas I see will simply not sell tickets. Too clever, too twisty, weak story, nothing much to say."

What If You Don't Have a Million Dollar Script?

There it is. Door slammed in all our faces. We can't get in without a great script, but our script isn't good enough. And we have to figure out for ourselves why. That's crazy. It's also true. But do you see the crack in this wall?

Obviously there are very few scripts written in any given year that are *Chinatown* wonderful. Yours probably isn't. Mine have never been. But there are quite a few really good scripts that are far enough away from being obviously great that most people can't see their potential. If that's yours, and if you have the aptitude, and if you've studied hard and practiced hard, that's a crack in the wall. Can you slip through? If you can find some way to get that almost great script improved in the shooting — with beautiful direction, inspiring performances, and a whole lot of luck — and if you refrain from making any of the truly dumb mistakes in the following pages — and if you jump through just the right hoops… yes. Absolutely. Someone is breaking in based on this very approach as you're reading these words. But how do we acquire the skills to take that near-great script and turn it into gold?

Just Do It. Is This Good Advice?

Someone told me how many copies, both licensed and unlicensed, of the popular editing program Final Cut Pro are in use. It ran to the hundreds of thousands. Many of these users will be happy to remain unpaid hobbyists. Some will lose interest. But many decide they have aptitude and try to take the shot. They'll spend significant money attempting it. It's come to be a fact that everything associated with the widespread longing in our culture to become a pop icon generates serious revenue — including the industry that publishes books like this one.

Thousands of film festivals charge entry fees averaging $50 each to hundreds of thousands of hopefuls. Do the math. Canon has sold literally millions of HDSLR cameras in the past five years. Corporate statements claim they've sold 50 million EF lenses alone. The explosion in "prosumer" filmmaking gear has been astounding, and extremely profitable. What are all these people doing with all this gear?

YouTube.

There are hundreds of thousands of people who describe themselves as filmmakers who spend enormous amounts of time creating movies for people to watch free of charge on YouTube. As of this writing there are 48 hours of video uploaded to the service every minute, resulting in nearly *eight years of content uploaded every day*. YouTube has millions of contributors.

Holy cow.

Most of these videos are by untrained hobbyists or cell phone cinematographers. They produce often very useful clips on topics like how to skin a deer or the always popular getting your cat to use the toilet. Most of what these enthusiasts do could hardly be described as directing mainstream movies — the object of this book. Watch a few YouTube videos. The camera tends to be shaky, the audio is that hollow on-board mic sound, very weak narrative thread, not much like anything you'd see at the theater or on TV. Which is not to say there may not be some wonderful moments captured in YouTube clips. But obviously, if a YouTube clip were saleable — it wouldn't be offered for free. And since making a living as a director is the object of this book, how do you move from the free world to the getting-paid one? Obviously by learning to make movies that people will pay to see. Where does the serious would-be filmmaker go to learn that? The majority are choosing film school.

Film School — Yes, No, And Why There Are So Many Of Them

There are entire books on film school, whether to go or not, how to pick one, what courses to take and so on. I have a few quick pointers based on having gone to film school myself, and having continued to teach off and on at schools of various types over time.

[With Rebecca Nield, William Peterson, Scott Mainwood, and Jon Anctil on the *CSI* set at Universal. Malcolm Oliver photo]

Film school. Spielberg and Coppola's generation started it. Today it seems there are more film schools than Starbucks. Ever wonder why?

There's a demand. It's a business.

There are a *lot* of people out there, cash in hand, wanting to become directors. Today there is scarcely a city of any size that doesn't boast at least one film school. The city I live in has *six* major ones. Teaching people about film generates a LOT of revenue. And who does this mushrooming growth industry turn to for teachers?

There are a ton of film workers who trained and thrived in the big film boom of 1980–2000. Many of them looking for work. Many of them are tired of humping cables, waiting in lunch lines, but are not old enough for retirement homes. There are also former content creators — producers, directors, writers — whose careers have stalled. They worked in a time when the video shelves needed filling, network TV could still finance movies with ad revenue, and there was no free content downloading to distract the paying audience. One top of all that, styles changed, the gear changed, the audience changed. I'm pretty sure I'm not going to get hired to direct another episode of *The Highlander*. Those days are gone, and so are those jobs.

That doesn't sound very encouraging. Come and learn from a bunch of guys who've lost the edge! Is everything my generation learned over the last few decades now obsolete? Obviously not. Just like the old guys who painted the pictures in the Louvre or Prado carried life-long wisdom about pigment, light, shadow and character, older working filmmakers — not just directors — know stuff. Valuable stuff.

It is a time-honored and noble tradition to pass on wisdom from one generation to the next. This is how our knowledge evolves, how we as a species evolve. Steven Soderbergh thanked teachers in his Oscar speech a few years ago. Thank you, Steven. I really appreciated that. Now you, the prospective student, needs to do some serious research about just *which* teachers Steven meant.

My Momma Told Me — You Better Shop Around

There are wonderful film schools where everyone is united in a mission to create amazing cinema and amazing filmmakers. These are places where there are clear goals, clear leadership, where highly competent people teach the specific skills they've learned over decades of practice, everyone pulls together, awards are won, students graduate into a life spent creating the stories we remember.

Let's find you one.

Remember, you're *paying* for this, often hundreds of dollars per class. Which teacher, which school, will give you your money's worth? For the would-be director, this is a very serious question.

I believe it is not unreasonable to expect a film school charging thousands of dollars to be able to train, within three or four years, a well-prepared, intelligent, hard-working student to become a working director, a paid content creator. Can anyone learn this? I don't know. I don't claim to have all the answers, but I do have some tips that might help you avoid what can otherwise be an appalling waste of time and life spirit.

[Watching film in class. Charles Wilkinson photo]

HOW TO CHOOSE YOUR FILM SCHOOL

Who have they taught? Before you sign on the dotted line, ask each school for a list of their graduates who are now established or working directors. IMDb search them. Some schools have a very good record in this area. Some not so much. If directing is what you want to learn, find a school that legitimately has produced currently working directors.

Above or below the line? There are films schools that are run by former sound mixers, make-up artists, and so on. They're often really good at teaching sound mixing, make-up, and so on.

Current faculty? Is this a school where the key faculty members are rewarded for staying current by making their own films? Schools like this pride themselves on producing award-winning, working film-makers. Good fit for you, the aspiring director.

Learning from success — or failure? Is there a climate of penetrating critical analysis at this school? Do the instructors step in with a gentle but firm hand? Are students guided with mature artistic authority and experience? Or are students primarily expected to learn from their own and each other's unguided failures? Surgeons, engineers, architects, airplane mechanics — all these are taught with a firm hand using <u>success</u> as the standard measure. In my experience, film is best taught this way. A tip: Before signing, go see their year-end show. If it's an ambitious, well-run affair featuring noteworthy films — you're home.

There it is. Four key questions. Next up, a few tips on what to do once you're sitting in class.

MAKING THE MOST OF FILM SCHOOL

Again, this is costing you a bundle. Don't settle for an instructor sitting you down in front of *Citizen Kane* for two hours. There's a lot to learn. Demand to be taught practical stuff like this:

Directing Actor Tip #283: When an actor or actress is reacting to the negativity in their scene — say there's a divorce or a crime of some sort — when they manifest negativity over a period of time they get uncomfortable to watch. Here's a tip. Ask them to *internalize* their pain. Grace under fire. Let the audience sense the pain they're going through, but to their scene partners — put on a bold face. Think about it — who likes someone who whines incessantly about their break-up? Who doesn't love the person who spares us their pain? That's a nugget of wisdom it took me years to learn. That's what you're paying me to teach you. Here's another:

Blocking Actors Tip #174: When you get in time trouble, block your master with half the actor's backs to camera. That way you can pick off half the close-ups with B Cam as you shoot the master, then turn around and get the rest of your coverage in one or two takes. Two set-ups and you've got the scene.

Knowledge like this is not poetry or rocket science. It's just a tiny example of a few of the thousands of things you're paying tuition for.

You May Have The Need For Speed — We Don't

Know the scene in *Top Gun* when Maverick and Goose are in their first class, where Mav boasts to Viper that he knows he's the best? Viper responds: *"That's pretty arrogant. I like that in a pilot."*

Know what? Few instructors with any kind of background appreciate attitude like that in a directing student. Filmmaking is a highly collaborative craft. Arrogance in a leader is just not an effective management tool. In any event, arrogance from someone who has yet to earn a single dollar from directing is just kind of amusing.

Yes, art is subjective and the judgements you receive on your work are only your instructor's opinion. But if they've had a good career creating content that people have paid to see, that's a pretty *informed* opinion, no? Here's a tip. If your instructor gives you a poor grade on a film — post it to YouTube. If it scores, say, 20,000 hits within a week — go to your instructor. A good one will revise your grade.

[Ohio University students watching films at the Athens Film Festival.
Charles Wilkinson photo]

Rosebud

One of the other very important things you'll get at film school is the chance to see a bunch of amazing films you've never heard of in an environment where you can learn something from them. Films that will expand your understanding of what the medium is capable of. Never seen *The Godfather* or *Apocalypse Now*? Or *Tootsie, Witness, Unforgiven, The Verdict, Bringing Up Baby, The Birth of a Nation*? What are you waiting for? These movies are amazing. They'll change your life.

I recently had a student show me the script she'd been slaving over for months. I read it, said it was a lot like a popular show from the '90s. She went and watched the show, then burned her script. It was a really good script too.

Here's yet another reason, a fun one. People in film have these secret handshake rituals; we often pepper our conversation with quotes from films. When a producer says to me something like: "*Help him? Help who?*" I must react with: "*Help the bombardier!*" If I don't, they know they're dealing with the uninitiated. [Quick — go watch Mike Nichols' *Catch-22*.] We're here because we LOVE movies — not only our own. For example, if anyone reading this doesn't get the "Rosebud" reference a few graphs back....

Pester Your Profs For Input

Film schools have curriculums. They are designed so the average student can keep up. Is that how you'd describe yourself? Average? Probably not. You probably want to do more than keep up. Your instructors are a resource you're paying for. Use them. Pester them for advice on a script, a cut, an idea even. That's where the real learning tends to happen.

And when you direct that student film, think about what your real objectives are. Your primary goal is to learn as much as possible. But you also want a good film at the end of the day. It's never too early to start winning student film festivals. There are books on this, so I won't elaborate too much. I just have a few notes on the stuff I see every day.

WHY DO STUDENT FILMS SUCK?

I have seen student films that challenged my very belief system. Marv Newland's student film *Bambi Meets Godzilla* remains my favorite animation of all time. Robert Boyd's student film *Labyrinth* inspired me to attend the film school he did. I had a student who used her short film to come out to her very conservative parents — it was heart-wrenching. But you have to admit, many student films simply don't work. The most common reason I see is that they're not *about* anything. Teen angst is a *subject*, not a story. If your story is about an average guy with a goofy bro roommate whose girlfriend is unhappy with their messy apartment — who cares?

Major tip: If your story can't convince a complete stranger to watch your movie by describing it with one 25-word sentence — they won't.

The second most common reason I see for student films that turn out poorly is that the student's reach exceeds their grasp. They try to tell stories that are too twisty, they use techniques that are too complex. Here's an analogy; there's a popular climbing mountain near where I live. Experienced climbers using pro gear scale the sheer rock face. Hikers climb the foot path. Quentin Tarantino is like an expert rock climber. He's learned how to use complex tools like pitons, carabineers, and rock bolts that enable him to make some bold moves — tools like time-shifting, extremely obnoxious characters in lead roles, never revealing the McGuffin in the brief case. These are his pitons, carabineers, and rock bolts. The student, on the other hand, is more like a hiker on the trail. You need different tools — a water bottle, sneakers, sunglasses, a hat. If you forget who you are and make the mistake of dragging rock climbing gear up the trail with you, not only will you misuse it — there's a good chance you won't make it to the top with your sneaker and t-shirt-clad friends. In other words, the more complex the story, the more skill it takes to tell, and the greater likelihood that a relative beginner will mess it up.

[Charles Wilkinson photo]

SIMPLE STORYTELLING TOOLS

Here's what Aristotle said about the basics of Western-style storytelling. *You need a sympathetic hero on a vital quest against insurmountable obstacles.* In addition, the ending needs to be *surprising but inevitable.* Choose a piece of material with those clear elements (sympathetic hero, vital quest, insurmountable obstacles, surprising but inevitable ending) and you'll likely do well. Attempt Tarantino's tricks — you'll likely not make it to the top of the hill. There are exceptions, of course. But here's a test: Watch a student film you feel doesn't work. Which one of those basic components didn't it have? It's almost certainly one of them.

A former student of mine did a TV interview the other day. She mentioned me — which was nice. Thanks, Dee. She said I told her that if she only remembered one thing from my class it had better be Aristotle's advice. She remembered it.

GRADES AND THE REAL WORLD

If you go to med school or law school and you get A+ grades all the way through, chances are almost certain you'll become a successful doctor or lawyer. Get A+ grades all the way through film school and your chances of becoming a working director are far from certain. So what value does a degree have?

Although no one will ever ask to see your school transcripts before offering you a directing job, a liberal arts degree has real value — both later on if you ever decide to get a real job, and now — in terms of your development as a human being. Most of the really important stuff you'll learn at film school will not happen in film class. Geography, Psychology, Art History, Modern Languages, Math — these things gave you *breadth.* They are your real education. Can you tell the difference between a Monet and a Caravaggio? Know what The New Deal was? How about The Reformation? I've personally needed to know these things to direct effectively. They have also enriched my life immeasurably. This stuff will *define* you if you let it.

GENTLEMEN, START YOUR ENGINES

Finally, once you graduate, it's my experience that you have a fairly narrow window within which to establish yourself as a promising young director. For a few years you'll have a willing crew of fellow graduates, access to a lot of free gear, access to a lot of advice from faculty who want to see you succeed, and the huge advantage of not yet having failed. Sci-Fi writer Robert Heinlein had a favorite character of his advise people that when they're in a gunfight, get a shot off *fast*. Chances are that even if you miss you'll distract your adversary long enough to take careful aim with shot #2. There's a certain amount of wisdom to that. I'm not saying make just anything. I am saying you've had between two and four years to get a viable project ready to shoot upon graduation. Know that if you blow this chance, it very likely won't come again.

The Graduate

When you've finally finished and it's grad time — go. Take your family. Wear the gown and cap. Toss it in the air along with everyone else. Do it *ironically* if you have to. But do it. Your parents and/or friends deserve some encouragement that this has all been worthwhile. Because you're about to prove that it has been.

Thoreau said it so well it bears repeating: "*If you have built castles in the air, your work need not be lost; that is where they should be. Now put foundations under them.*"

You've poured the concrete footings now — good start. What's next?

[Pablo the graduate. Charles Wilkinson photo]

chapter three

THE FIRST FILM

T hose of you who have already made that first commercial film, or maybe even dozens of them, might think that this is a chapter to skip. Stick around for a sec.

Many working and even established directors may come to a point where the phone stops ringing. Maybe you passed on too many shows you thought were dumb. Maybe you were too difficult. Maybe you had a streak of bad luck. Maybe you got lost in drugs or alcohol for a while. Could be a thousand reasons. But your phone's not ringing now and it may not again without some help from you.

Are you going to take this? Is that all you got? Are the guys who won't hire you anymore right? Are you washed up? Finished? I don't think so. If you made it to the chequered flag once, I'm betting you still have something in the tank. If only they'd give you one more chance. But they won't? So do it on your own. If you have something to say that you believe is worth saying — say it. Here's how.

Everyone does a first film. Ironically, as we adapt to a constantly changing world, some of us have to do a number of "first" films. If your phone isn't ringing for whatever reason, you have to either invent or re-invent yourself. You're all facing that first film syndrome, and to say the ground rules have changed in the past decade is like saying the Titanic took on some water.

For their 1984 debut film *Blood Simple*, the Coen Brothers wrote a truly amazing script, then raised just under a million dollars from a large number of lawyers, dentists, and so forth. That was then. But remember, this was a time when the risks were lower — home video and specialty TV were expanding. There were far fewer films, hence much less competition. But they needed more money. The equipment and production materials were very expensive.

Although it's becoming less common, first-time directors still raise relatively large amounts and shoot in relatively traditional ways: large crews, lots of gear, industry standard practices. But increasingly, money like this is hard to raise unless the first-timer has "elements" in place that will reduce investor risk: stars.

Everyone has a story about how so-and-so got their script to Natalie Portman's brother, who got her to read it and say yes to working for scale. It happens. Just not very often. Stars work really hard to win that status. They know in their bones how fleeting it can be. One or two really bad pictures and they're gone. So why would a star risk all this on your low-budget picture? Well, if you've won a zillion student film festivals, if you have an absolutely world-changing script. Oh, *that* again.

By all means, try to get a star to read your script. Just know that there are tens of thousands of people out there who spend years trying and failing. And know also that there are other ways.

Who's in *The Blair Witch Project*? Who's in *Open Water* or *Napoleon Dynamite* or *District 9*? Movies without stars can work. And working without stars saves you all the related costs: first-class travel, decent hotels and transportation, security, a trailer, proper hair, wardrobe and make-up, and on and on. Non-stars are *campers*. They'll get down and dirty with you in the trenches.

On the technical side, production costs have quite simply plummeted. So what's stopping you?

[Shooting w/7D on *Peace Out*. Pablo Wilkinson photo]

Making Movies Doesn't Cost Much Anymore

Amazingly, the would-be working director can now kickstart their career by self-producing a viable feature movie that wins festivals and makes money. The so-called "prosumer" production equipment available today makes it entirely possible to produce a viable feature movie for less than the cost of a decent used car. Again, check out YouTube. There are thousands of trailers for feature movies made by people like that girl in Ohio. These movies are called "self-financed" or "micro-budget" films.

This sounds easy. Why doesn't everyone make one of these? The answer is that many people do. I know of a number of young directors who have invested 2–3 years of their lives and all their and their friend's resources making a movie. The downside with many of these films is that it's hard getting anyone to want to see them. Many have been unable to sell for $1. And such films often prove unable to get even one festival to accept them.

Gee. This suddenly doesn't sound so hot. Investing all those resources, all that time, and then — nothing. Clearly there are ways to go about doing this.

Based on past experience and the things I've seen recently on the festival circuit with my own films, I'm starting to believe that the default strategy for the majority of first-time would-be working directors is becoming the self-financed film. Externally financed first films will clearly continue to be made. Either way, a new era of small-budget filmmaking has begun. The following pages focus on the self-financed micro-budget film. But the notes are equally valid for those lucky enough to win some external investment.

THE SELF-FINANCED FILM

Super Size Me. Clerks. Hollywood Shuffle. These successful films are all described as being "self-financed." What does that even mean? Director James Cameron famously invested a good portion of his fees for *Titanic* when it went over budget. Is that self-financing? A good way to explain this might be to describe what self-financing *isn't*.

The conventional model for film financing involves a filmmaker convincing one or more film production companies to advance the money needed to make the film against potential future profits. The production companies do this because they believe the film will make money. Or, in the case of state-financed cultural agencies, they'll grant funding because the film meets their cultural criteria (encouraging tourism to Bulgaria, for example).

Key here is that *they* decide.

We've all heard countless stories of filmmakers spending years trying unsuccessfully to raise financing for their film. Why? Because the people they were asking for money said no. Why? Because they didn't think the film would make the money back (or serve the cultural goals of the state funders). Who are these people? What do they look for? Are they always, or even often, right?

Nope. Proof is, most movies lose money. Does that mean that most of the people saying no to you are wrong most of the time? No. There are a million projects out there that these folks *should* say no to.

But it does mean that most green-lit projects fail to turn a profit.

So how does Hollywood stay in business? They try to make blockbusters that make so much money that the losers are subsidized. Also, even a big money-loser at the box office can be quite profitable in TV and foreign sales if it's been the beneficiary of a massive ad campaign.

Independent films that do not have huge ad campaigns and fail to catch on with the public are certain money-losers. Unfortunately, that's where we all have to start, and most people with money fear the beginners are probably not going to make any of their money back for them.

So, these people who advance money to filmmakers to make movies try to cover their bets, to reduce their risks. They do this by insisting the films they invest in have stars and/or stories that have some attractive quality that people will pay to see, even if the movie itself is not so hot. If you need under five million and you get Johnny Depp or Brad Pitt to say yes to you, or get the exclusive rights to the Michael Jackson story, or the hunt for Osama Bin Laden — you'll get financed.

But what if you don't want to do a story like this? What if you don't want to spend two years hounding Brad Pitt's brother-in-law so he'll read your screenplay? What if *you* want to decide what will work?

A self-financed film is one where the filmmaker has the power to green-light the project.

Have you got a project you believe in and think you can produce for virtually no money? There are some powerful reasons to self-finance. And some powerful reasons not to.

THE PROS

It's great to not have to deal with years of people saying no.

It's great to have 100% creative control.

Gambling is a lot of fun, and this is potentially a *big* casino.

Do this and you will have directed a movie.

THE CONS

The industry gatekeepers know a thing or two. Maybe your idea isn't fully developed.

Maybe *you're* not ready yet.

If you make a terrible first movie, it sticks to you — movie #2 becomes a lot harder.

You'll need a ton of favors to finish this. You only get to ask once. Blow your favors on a lame project and they're gone forever.

The time and money you spend will take years to make up.

The odds against this working are, frankly — *astronomical*.

So should you do this? In Sunday School when I was a kid I remember the teacher saying once that we have the right to work, but not the right to expect the <u>fruits</u> of that labor. I always wondered what that meant. After decades of hard work I think I know now. I think most working directors make movies because we love the work itself — irrespective of the reward. The prestige, the money — all that passes so quickly. What we're left with is a sense of a job well done. Like I imagine a doctor feels who's delivered a lot of babies. Or a lawyer who's won justice for years of innocent clients.

I see so many people in this business striving to "make it." Like if they can just get <u>one</u> thing to happen — get a video to go viral or get a script read by Matt Damon, that this *magic* thing will happen to transform them into a brand new person. Think about it for a minute. If the friends you have right now don't respect you for what you are, do you honestly think Rihanna and Justin Bieber will see a different person in you once you've "made it"? They can't. You're you.

Here's a test: imagine all the incredibly hard work that stands between you and getting that first film made. Imagine on the night you finish it your house burns down destroying every trace of the film. Are you devastated and outraged at this tragic and colossal waste of time and money? Or can you laugh and move on? If you can do the work and love it without promise of reward — my advice is take the leap and do it.

OK, having said that, and assuming we're all doing this for love, we want to find the most effective way that we can keep doing it for love, over and over. That needs strategy.

What Must You Actually Accomplish With This Film?

Most self-financed films fail to enable their maker to more easily make their next film. Why? The defining feature of most self-financed films I've seen are that they were made because the filmmaker could. They had a camera, some friends who could act, crew, drive, cook. They ended up with a movie — but they were no closer to their real goal. They failed in part because they did not first consider the much more important question — what am I actually trying to accomplish?

What kind of a question is that? You want to be famous and rich and date stars and have your high school teachers admit they were wrong and… See what I mean? Some of this may happen. But even with a really successful film, most of it won't. Can we separate what you need from what you might *want*?

Have you seen the Bennett Miller film *Moneyball*? It details how an economics grad re-defined the game of baseball by realizing that winning games is about *getting guys on base*. That approach took a losing team close to winning the pennant and revolutionized the sport. The hopeful young film director needs that kind of outside-the-box thinking. So, what's your objective? Simple.

You want the people who finance films to take you seriously as a director.

For the would-be working director — that is your one and only practical goal. And how do you make these people take you seriously? There are only two ways:

> Make waves.
> Make money.

That's it.

Example: Back in 1981, a guy who was an AD on slasher films and a guy who was a typist at a department store wrote a script, got a bunch of people to invest various small amounts, spent the next several years shooting and cutting, and released the first of what was to become one of the most outstanding bodies of work in the modern cinema. The guys? Joel and Ethan Coen. Their objective? I don't know the brothers, so I can only speculate. Quite simply, *Blood Simple* planted the Coen brother's feet firmly on the first steps of the path to creating a string of immensely thought-provoking, intelligent, and profitable movies. How did they do that?

Blood Simple made waves. After a slow start, it got very good reviews, it attracted a great deal of attention and admiration on the festival circuit. The festival buzz secured for the film a U.S. theatrical run that brought out paying customers. *Blood Simple* made money.

Make waves. Make money.

If it's as obvious as that, why doesn't everybody do it? Obvious does not equal easy. One obvious way to get rich is to discover gold. Try it some time. But just as there is a path one follows to discover gold, there is a path one can follow to make waves and money with a self-financed film. Let's talk about that path.

RECIPE FOR THE SUCCESSFUL SELF-FINANCED FILM

Ingredients:
1. Knowledge
2. The Story
3. The Cast
4. The Crew
5. The Gear
6. The Location/s
7. The Money (it always takes at least some)
8. Dos & Don'ts
9. Finishing Touches

1. KNOWLEDGE

As much knowledge as you can acquire is barely enough. Returning to *Blood Simple*, I'm always struck when studying the Coen Brothers' beginnings by how much prep they did. I don't mean storyboards and shot lists, although they did that too. I mean deep study of genre, the history of related literature, painting, and film, recent developments in technique, the work of others, market conditions, and so on. It makes a great story to talk about a couple of random guys from nowhere working nothing jobs who suddenly get lucky. But legendary film mogul Sam Goldwyn had a great quote that speaks to this:

"The harder I work, the luckier I get."

The Coens worked hard, just like another "overnight success" worked hard — Robert Rodriguez. Google him. See how his early life was essentially a 24/7 film school experience driven by hard work and obsession. How about that other overnight success — Quentin Tarantino, a guy who by his own admission grew up without any of the perks most of us associate with childhood: no cars, girls, proms, vacations, hobbies. Just a 24/7 devotion to acquiring all the knowledge available on cinema.

Yes, these people are also very smart and very lucky. But the good news is that the same information they studied is just sitting there, waiting for you.

2. THE STORY

There was a 1984 Wendy's hamburger chain ad with three old ladies demanding to know of a competitor's burger: "Where's the beef?" In these vegan times it's tempting to revise this to "Where's the tofu?" But tofu doesn't pack much of a wallop — and that's the point. Can we settle on *protein*? Where's the protein?

Why must we watch this movie of yours? Why *must* we. Not why *might* we. *Napoleon Dynamite* was just crazy — we had to watch. *Garden State, The Blair Witch Project, Hard Candy, Open Water.* We *had* to watch those films. Tarantino's protein in the famous *Reservoir Dogs* "Like A Virgin" scene is outrageous obscenity and profanity coupled with clever humor. Audiences howled with laughter. That's protein.

So where's yours?

I see a lot of scripts about that non-descript guy with no particular skills or features who lives in a messy apartment with a bro, whose girlfriend resents their friendship and hatches some plan to split them up. This is a subject, not a story. *Where's the protein?*

Remember the eight years' worth of content uploaded to YouTube *every day*? People have only so much time to spend watching anything. If they can stream Danny Boyle's latest film for a few dollars on Netflix, why would they watch a film you made? That's easy.

You're *you*.

Everyone has at least one distinct story inside. There is a story no one on earth knows as much about as you. Find some way of getting that on paper. Then, when you've got your script, get advice. I have a set of people I've cultivated over a lifetime. Unless they say my script is incredibly good, it likely isn't. Everyone knows people who are smart and articulate. Tell your movie story to them. If they aren't hanging off every word, you have work to do. If your story doesn't attract real interest, filming it won't make it any better.

A word on the "I don't want to reveal what my movie is about because someone might steal it" thing. They probably won't. (In my entire career I've had one script stolen — a story I wrote in a period of despair — about a beautiful but brilliant shepherd from the third world who comes to the U.S. to confront the evil corporate guys who are polluting her land. I ask you, *who would steal something this bad?* But when the production deal fell apart, steal it they did. And they added a <u>dance</u> component. Seriously. It turns out this hot shepherd is an amazing dancer as well. (The lightweights who stole the script were rewarded with a dump truck full of karma — the show tanked, and the "filmmakers" were sentenced to years of producing shows far worse than this one. Funny how that works.) Very few movie ideas are ever stolen. It's a risk, yes. So is passing the car in front of you in a race. Taking *calculated* risks is how you win.

A log line is a great place to start. What's a log line? Wikipedia says:

"A log line or logline is a brief summary of a television program or film, often providing both a synopsis of the program's plot, and an emotional 'hook' to stimulate interest."

The most basic function of a log line is you telling me what your movie is about in a way that makes me have to see it. Want to go see a movie tonight about this little kid who is an orphan and he's interested in mechanical things and he meets this old guy who shares his interests? Me either. That's not a very good way to describe Martin Scorsese's *Hugo*. A good log line makes people want to see the movie. It must be a clear answer to "Where's that protein?"

Here's a great test. Imagine you're trying to get someone to come watch your movie tonight — someone who has a dream date with this amazing person, and that date is 100% likely to end *well*. What can you tell them about your movie that will make them momentarily consider cancelling the date? That's how high the bar is.

Can I Tell My Whole Movie?

Why not? Legendary film editor Ralph Rosenblum — in his must-read book on editing, *When The Shooting Stops... The Cutting Begins* — tells of how writer/actor/director Mel Brooks (*Blazing Saddles, The Producers, Young Frankenstein*) would act out his entire screenplay, performing all of the characters, doing all of the voices, just for the entertainment of the editing room crew. Here's a man who loves storytelling.

3. THE CAST

I saw a super interesting film at a festival last month. Ingrid Veninger's *i am a good person / i am a bad person*. The film was a model for the micro-budget filmmaker. The film was shot on location in Toronto, England, Paris, and Berlin — all venues Ingrid was being flown to for festival screenings of her previous film (so free airfare). Her remarkable film cost less than most Hollywood films spend on bottled water. There were only four main speaking parts plus a handful of smaller day players. And yet, watching the audience during the screening it was clear that we all just followed the story, regardless of the resources used to produce it. Once the lights went out it was quite simply — a movie.

[Director Ingrid Veninger with crew and cast in Paris. Hallie Switzer photo]

Cast could be your major production expense. Even assuming your actors (and crew) are working for what we call "deferred compensation" — i.e., no cash up front. So why is having a tiny cast like this is so important on a no-budget show?

Back in the studio days people used to joke about D.W. Griffith's big "cast of thousands" epics having coffee and donuts as their biggest expense. On a self-financed show, coffee and donuts actually *could* be your biggest expense if you're not careful. People eat. They take up space in cars, planes. That costs money. Less people, less money.

Backing up a bit, why would a decent actor work on your movie for nothing? The answer? They won't. No one worth anything works for nothing. Remember that. You get what you pay for. So how do you pay good people when you have no money? With something other than money. What do these people value that you can give them? A chance to work toward achieving their objective. An opportunity to invest in their career. This holds true for everyone on your cast and crew.

You may cast actors who have worked on real movies in supporting roles. These are capable performers who aren't getting starring roles. They want starring roles to prove themselves. You have starring roles to offer. Deal. Neither of you are doing the other a favor. Or rather, both of you are.

But be very very clear, right from the start. This is wilderness camping. You expect your actors to carry cases, roll up cables, drive themselves, wear their own wardrobe, do their own hair and makeup, agree to eat whatever chow you can rustle up. They have to agree to that in advance. You cannot afford even one single-shot cappuccino at Starbucks. Not one.

But here's the thing. If you have done your background study. If you have a script that is bordering on the outrageously entertaining. If you assemble all the other elements you need to do this — you are giving these actors an amazing opportunity. They give you a month or so of their life. You give them a shot at moving up. That is an exchange of high value. Both of you need to treat it with respect.

4. THE CREW

I directed my first feature film with a crew of three — the DP, the soundman, and myself. I had a cast of two, plus day players. Although it has moments, it's far from a good film. But what is wrong with it *has nothing whatever to do with the resources I had.* The *script* was awful. If it had been better, if I could go back now and re-write it, I believe the film might have been a real success — *with a three-man crew and a two-person cast.*

[With DP Tobias Schliessler on my first student film. Charles Wilkinson photo]

Script aside, in many ways I enjoyed the experience of making that film as much as anything I've worked on. Small production is wonderful. So who do you absolutely need?

You need a gifted director of photography, someone with a great sense of vision, a deep background studying the visual arts, and an ability to find ways of shooting beautifully with available light. The brilliant Tobias Schliessler (*Friday Night Lights, Dreamgirls, Battleship*) shot my first shows. Why available light? Because lights require money. They take up room in the van, they require power and people to set them up. You have none of these things.

Thankfully the new HD cameras are so sensitive to low light that shooting without lights — depending on your story — has become entirely feasible. I watched a shoot-out on Zakudo.com a while back comparing 35mm film to the various HDSLRs. Film still had the advantage on dynamic range. But one of the digitals could shoot at over 100,000 ISO! The DP remarked that it is becoming possible to shoot a moonlit scene using only moonlight. That's just amazing. And it shows no signs of letting up. As I write this the new multi-layered chip technology has expanded HD video's dynamic range to ten stops of exposure! This compares very favorably with 35mm film. It even exceeds the human eye under certain conditions. So the key skill you'll be needing in your DP is an ability to recognize where the reality looks good already — not how to load in tons of gear to create a false reality.

You must also find a talented sound mixer. Sound is nearly as critical as picture. Particularly with dialogue, anything less than crystal clear, close-mic'd audio could doom your show. So no, you can't use the on-board mic. In my conversations with festival programmers I've learned that bad audio is one of the most common reasons a film is rejected for festival play. It's right up there with hyper-shakey hand-held "soccer mom" camerawork.

The third man is you, the director. Am I seriously recommending that you make a feature film with a crew of three? Yes, I am. With the right script, crew and gear it's not only possible, it's fun, and in any event, can you afford more?

I see this curious syndrome in some of the students I work with where they're not happy unless they have a crew of forty and every piece of gear imaginable on the set of their five-minute film. They think it's how the big boys do it. They're right. But it's not how the big boys learned to do it. It's not how they got in the door.

5. THE GEAR

People write entire books about what gear to choose. I'm not sure the would-be director needs to read them. Gear today is so uniformly good that — to the director — it's all good. Don't worry too much about it. You won't be needing much. An HDSLR camera (great for stealth); several fast, hi-quality lenses; a good tripod; you may need a hand-held rig if there's lots of that in the plan. Avoid building the HD-SLR into an add-on Frankenstein. If you need a matte box and follow focus and monitor — this may be just too much gear for the kind of speed you'll be needing. Consider a more conventional camera.

[Ben Lichty shoots a scene with Hallie Switzer on the Paris Metro.
  Ingrid Veninger photo]

You'll need as many mics as you have actors. Radio mics are great and (under the right conditions) can save a boom operator. A small digital recorder like the Zoom H4N is sufficient. HDSLR audio as of this writing is still evolving, so you'll want to record dual system — that is, record sound on a separate unit and sync it up later.

You'll need a good headset — the type with big cans that cover the ears.

You'll need enough data cards.

You'll need a laptop with tons of outboard drive space. We also carry an external BluRay burner so we can have a "hard copy" of everything in case there's a huge failure.

For post you'll need a desktop computer with a very powerful processor, NLE software, two monitors, near field speakers, and reams of storage. I used 8TB on my last show.

6. THE LOCATION/S

When I look at the shows that I and other directors I know do for very low budgets, one thing really sticks out — location. If you can find a single location that is perfect for your story and perfect for production — some place you can virtually live at until you're finished — you're way ahead.

It's not unusual in this no-budget world to find an amazing location that then inspires a story. Imagine the story that could come out of an abandoned factory or ghost town. This happened on all my lower-budget work. Still does. Place is always a prominent feature. Hollywood often creates 100% of their amazing locations digitally with CGI. *You* must find places that look that amazing as is.

My very first commercial film was shot 100% in a closed federal prison. It was perfect — we loaded gear in and out once. We put all our energy on the screen. My first feature, the three-man crew one, was shot in a very small town where we virtually had the "keys to the city." Seriously. We shot car chases at dawn in the downtown business district without any permits or traffic control. The local police even acted in the movie, in uniform, with their cars — for free. I directed the pilot for a popular TV series at a bankrupt mountain resort where we not only shot 100% of the show, but the entire cast and crew stayed there under the one roof (and had a wrap party every night of the shoot — sigh). These shows all had stunning production value — far more than their meager budgets would suggest.

[Bridge, Paris, shooting an afternoon scene. Hallie Switzer photo]

7. THE MONEY (IT ALWAYS TAKES AT LEAST SOME)

Yes, you need *some* money. At least for gas, food, and lodging. The costs associated with self-financed films tend mostly to be living costs. And although you'd be spending this money anyway, all the time you spend working on this is time not spent earning money.

Where can you find this money? Some filmmakers pool their resources with cast and crew. I don't think that's real attractive — *what, you want me to pay so I can work for free?* Some directors sell their stuff — houses, cars, etc. Better. A small group of family and friends, doctors and lawyers? If they can afford to be patrons of the arts, if they understand that there is virtually no chance they'll get their money back, then fine. Then, if your show is that one in a million that makes money, they'll be pleasantly surprised.

There are some neat new trends in self-financing worth mentioning. There are websites that give the filmmaker a chance to raise money from hundreds, even thousands, of small, online fan/investors. You pitch your idea, name a dollar value you wish to raise, then people start investing (or not). There's usually a provision that if you don't raise the full amount, no one has to invest — an all or nothing clause. Then, the idea is that you repay from any film earnings. There are some films that have raised a lot this way. Check it out.

However you do it, self-financing is not free. But if you have the story, the skills, and the resources, the self-financed film can be the best investment the would-be or temporarily unemployed working director can ever make.

8. DOS & DON'TS
Even with a great script, a good skill set, and the required resources, stuff can still go wrong. Here are a few notes I've taken from my and other's experiences on this battlefield.

Do....
∾ Do be honest–ish (see next note).

∾ Do pretend to that bus driver or police officer that you're just a tourist taking stills.

∾ Do be responsible. Other filmmakers will follow you. Please don't make it harder for us.

∾ Do bet the worst. Assume the picture will go nowhere. If that's acceptable, do it. If you're betting the money for your grandma's operation, don't.

∾ Do plan everything.

∾ Do cultivate mentors. You're going to need all the good advice you can get.

Don't....
∾ Don't lie to or otherwise abuse your cast and crew. Lose them, you're done.

∾ Don't over-crew or have hangers-on. A one-van unit is way more than twice as fast as a two-van unit.

∾ Don't undervalue people's time, just because you're not paying cash for it.

∾ Don't waste resources chasing "production value." Accept that this won't look as good as *Avatar*. It's the story they'll come for, not the look.

∾ Don't have sex with your actors or crew. Small unit shows are a pressure cooker. Sex makes it way worse. Wait for the wrap party, or preferably after the party, if possible.

∾ Don't tolerate *ongoing* disunity in your cast or crew. Creative debate is vital, but fire people if they just don't share the vision. Otherwise — a living hell awaits.

∾ Don't drag it out. Every day you procrastinate makes it that much harder to finish the film. Get it out there. Move on.

9. FINISHING TOUCHES

So often a filmmaker who stressed out on every detail in production treats post-production with relative indifference. Post makes or breaks your vision. And unlike back in the day when editing cost money, anyone with a solid desktop computer, a quality NLE (non-linear editing system like Avid or Final Cut), and a robust skill set can finish a theatrical-quality feature film virtually free of charge. A few notes.

Music: Involve your composer early on. Do not under any circumstances fall for the traditional composer line about "I'll start when you have picture lock." That's code for: There are other projects I'm doing right now. Yes, it's way more work to score scenes that change. But music is so integral to the movie that you must have it as you move forward. I often score my own films so it's not as big a deal arguing with myself on this. If I'm using a composer I'll take a less-experienced one any day, one who'll commit more time to the project, over an experienced one who wants to waltz into the final mix with his/her tracks.

Don't waste a lot of time dealing with record labels to try and get your favorite indie band's music for your show. The band may be totally into it. But their label guys are often a different story. I've found record label people are often difficult people for the low-budget filmmaker to deal with. These are the people who advised Led Zeppelin not to go to Woodstock. But obviously, indie songs can make a real difference to a certain kind of film, so it might be worth the effort. If you have someone you can push this task off onto, great.

The Soundtrack: This is a simple tip that so many young filmmakers miss. *You cannot create a soundtrack using headphones.* You must have "near field" speakers. Near fields closely replicate what the viewer in a theater setting will hear. Headphones replicate a scenario where your audience is on stepladders with their ears pressed up against the speakers. Near fields aren't cheap, but they're cheaper than all those stepladders.

Audience Testing: From rough cut on many filmmakers find it a good idea to test the film often. We usually burn a BluRay every Friday night and arrange a screening on the weekend, inviting carefully selected people whose opinions we trust and respect. There's no substitute for watching a movie with a crowd. It just feels different. Hard to explain. It's as if you astral trip into the audience's brains, you feel the movie from their POV. You're going to do this sooner or later. Better now when you can do something about it than at the premiere when you suddenly realize the whole thing is too slow.

Rough Cuts To Festivals? Depends. You only get one shot. If you send something too rough it will get rejected and that's it for that festival. But if the film is essentially done but needs color correction, titles and sound work, and if the festival is important like Cannes, Sundance or Toronto, it may be worth taking the chance.

Caution: Do not let screeners out of your hand unless you can totally trust the firm or person. Particularly if your film identifies with a social justice or environmental issue of any kind. For some reason the people who fight for these causes often seem to think there's such thing as justifiable copyright violation. There's a real risk they'll post your work to the Internet, not realizing they've just destroyed your chances for festivals and TV broadcast — and thus destroyed your film's chances to help advance their cause.

Walking Away: Know that no film is ever finished — they're only abandoned. One of the big problems with the self-financed film is that the director is not being pressured by the financiers, the studio, the network to finish it. The work can go on forever. A finished and delivered film with minor flaws is infinitely better than one that's never finished. Set a deadline and honor it.

It's finished. Amazing. You made the movie. How cool is that?

Get your water wings. It's time to make some waves.

[HDSLR production gear on *Peace Out*. Tina Schliessler photo]

chapter four

MAKING WAVES: THE FESTIVAL CIRCUIT

There was a time, not long ago, when relatively few movies were made. It was not uncommon to see news items in local papers about some local person who had *actually made one*. It was news. It isn't any more. If you make it, they won't automatically come. Competition for eyeballs is extreme. Yet, some small films get seen. How?

[Festival Pass Vancouver International Film Festival.
Charles Wilkinson photo]

The film festival circuit has become the main point of entry for the small film filmmaker. Film festivals are to the small film filmmaker what President's Choice is to the small commodity producer. Let's say you manufacture an excellent line of granola. There is almost no way a small firm can compete for shelf space with General Foods. But if you can get your product endorsed (re-branded) by President's Choice, you suddenly get shelf space and a fair shot at competing.

Same thing with movies. If you make a movie, you are in direct, head-to-head competition with Universal's half-billion-dollar *Battleship* epic opening this weekend. As a customer, I have $12 and a free evening. I can either see the extravaganza I've been shouted at about in a several hundred million dollar ad campaign — a movie I'm pretty sure will have an amazing look and terrific FX, even if the story kind of blows. Or I can see a sensitive no-budget movie about relationships that I've heard nothing about and featuring no stars. Why would I chose yours?

Just because your movie cost $25,000 to make and *Battleship* cost $300 million doesn't make me want to see yours. *It's not like ticket prices are based on a percentage of the production budget.* All movie tickets cost the same. Universal reached me by buying my attention. You don't have that option. Is there a way for you to get my attention? Happily, there is.

So I'm lined up to see *Battleship*. I see your poster. It has those leafy festival laurels all over it.

I examine them. There are so many festivals it's hard to know. My feeling is that if a film has achieved festival success — period — it's worth a second look. If your film has been an official selection at Cannes, Sundance, and Toronto, that alone gets me out of the *Battleship* line-up into yours. That's just me, though. The programmers at those three festivals often individually select movies I'm not crazy about, but when all three choose the same film, that's as close as it gets to a guarantee for me. But some viewers need more. Go closer.

Study the poster and you may (hopefully) see some quotes. Things like: *"Once in a generation a film comes along that rearranges the very DNA of life as we know it. This is one such dark and disturbing masterpiece...."*

Now if this quote is attributed to Irving Mulch of the *Podunk Farm News*, it probably won't cut much ice with you. But if it's from a credible national source like *The New York Times*, for example it's going to convince a lot of people to buy that ticket. Again, most reviews for smaller films originate at festivals.

WHICH FESTIVALS SHOULD YOU ENTER?

There are quite simply thousands of film festivals around the world. Why? The solid ones are run by cinephiles who bring the wonderful cinema of the world to their cities, amazing films their fellow enthusiasts would otherwise never see. This describes the majority of festivals. Of course there are those run as a profit-making enterprise by floundering filmmakers who find irresistible the prospect of a few thousand hopeful filmmakers sending them $50 each for an entry fee, then getting a free community hall and free judges, handing out a paper certificate and running. Either way, most film festivals charge money for entry fees — a lot of money. And you as a filmmaker have to choose which ones you stand the best chance at. How do you do that?

Research it. I do, for every film I make. Because it changes all the time. In a nutshell here's what I've learned by sometimes happy, but sometimes painful, and always expensive, experience:

The top-tier fests are pretty much mandatory — Cannes, Sundance, and Toronto, a few others. If your film is a documentary, then Hot Docs and IDFA in Amsterdam.

Top festivals have premiere requirements. Don't allow a minor festival in Guelph, Ontario, to screen your film if you're hoping for TIFF. Don't put your movie online until the festival run is over. Each fest has different rules. Check them.

There are a number of online resource sites that list the top fests in the world. Check them out. Many of the writers have done solid research.

Enter festivals that espouse the same ideas your film does. A film with gay/lesbian plot lines is more likely to be selected at a gay/lesbian festival. A film about the Paris-Dakar Rally is less likely to be chosen by a green fest.

Consider smaller festivals in places you'd really like to visit. Seriously. We entered *Peace Out* in the Available Light Film Festival in the Yukon. It turned out to be a wonderful experience, it helped the film, I met some new filmmakers, and I got to go dog-sledding!

[Mushing in the Yukon at ALFF. Julia Ivanova photo]

It's important to remember that we're not just in this for the work. It's supposed to be fun, and unusual places inspire unusual new stories.

Set a budget for how much you can afford to spend on entry fees. It can really add up. Keep meticulous track of your entries and the outcomes. Note the festivals that rejected you courteously — those are keepers. Note those that took your money and didn't bother sending you a formal rejection — never again.

Know when to quit. If you've entered your film in 100 festivals (at a cost of $5,000) and you've been rejected at every one, maybe it's time to bail and start thinking about one of my favorite lines: "*See the film that no film festival dared to program…*."

HOW DO YOU ENTER?

All festivals used to have time-consuming entry processes. You'd fill out the application, compile a long list of promotional materials, the screeners, a trailer, and so on. You'd bundle it all up, include a check, and courier it off. Some still do that. But, increasingly, most festivals subscribe to the couple of online festival entry sites that streamline the process:

Withoutabox.com
Shortfilmdepot.com

Basically, the filmmaker completes an online application only once, you upload all the required materials, then select the festivals you wish to enter. You pay via credit card or PayPal. You send your screener to the actual festival. Done.

The lists of what materials festivals want are easy to find online. What needs to be discussed here is quality. The impression your film will create is initially based on the quality of the promotion materials you generate. First glance, these materials ARE your film. An arresting one-sheet with an eye-catching image and thought-provoking cut line sets up a positive expectation — just as something lame sets up a negative one. A clear and lucid synopsis describing the film is mandatory. Include the official laurel logos from any significant festivals you've been accepted at. Your promo art really needs to excel.

One thing I've noticed some film students struggle with is the fact that studio movie artwork is almost entirely irrelevant to small films. They'll show me a poster with a random gentleman standing in front of a 10-year-old Chevy Cavalier. The title will be something like: *The Event*. And I'll go — wtf? They'll point out the poster for Clint Eastwood's *Gran Torino*. There's a guy — I got that. There's a car — check. Cool title — yup. And I say — But it's CLINT EASTWOOD!

Go online and seek out promo material for other films in your genre. Does your material measure up? All the artwork you create for this project — the one-sheets, the postcards, the posters, the box art — all of it must answer this one critical question: Why should we come see this movie? Here are the possible answers:

~ See this movie because it's an amazing look at a subject you care a lot about.

∾ See this movie because respected film festivals say to.

∾ See this movie because respected critics say to.

If your artwork doesn't say that — festival programmers who might otherwise like your film may well reject it. Why?

WHAT FESTIVALS ARE LOOKING FOR

There are festival directors who intentionally program super "arty" but deeply unpopular films they believe in — just for the sheer integrity of it. There are not very many festival directors like this. Festivals live or die by *people in seats*. It's how they prove their relevance, how they make rent and payroll, how they stay alive. Your package — your poster, your artwork, your blurb, your cutline, your synopsis — is really all they have to sell the public on.

Is there a way to convince festival directors that you can fill seats? Yes. Increasingly festivals ask you to submit links to all the friends and supporters of your film. My current one, *Peace Out*, is about environmental issues. Quite a few environmental groups have come out in support of it. By linking them to the project, we're telling festival directors that we have a lot of friends who will buy tickets. So who has a vested interest in seeing the ideas in your film get promoted? Say your movies is about a guy who loves drag racing, but realizes the sport can't survive in a carbon-averse world, so he builds the world's first green dragster? You've got interest in the environmental community, in the car racing community, possibly in the Harley crowd, there's possible tie-ins with race suppliers, the police, driver's ed programs — the possibilities are extensive. Be creative. Get those groups on your side. Fill that house.

Because please believe me — it is HARD to fill a theater. You can spend weeks promoting, you can do tons of press, only to find a half-full house. Getting out a crowd is extremely time consuming. The big consolation is that sooner or later, if your picture warrants it, word of mouth will kick in and you can sit back and watch it roll on under its own steam. Until then it's just hard work. We recently had a screening in Fort St. John, a small northern city. When I saw the room, I was apprehensive — 400+ seats at

$12 a ticket. I went for a walk before the show. The organizer — Danielle — had put 11"x17" posters for the film in almost every window in the downtown core. Hundreds of handbills — each one involving a conversation with and permission from the merchant. It was complete overkill. When we got back to the theater it was standing room only. That's what it took.

One of the materials you'll be asked for is a trailer. There are great resources around for how to cut a good trailer. My notes:

1. It needs to be online and in HD. Vimeo, YouTube, and/or Withoutabox/IMDb.

2. Short and sweet, to the point, and protein-packed.

3. There's no reason not to have several versions available. Short to hook them, longer to reel them in.

ONCE YOU'RE IN

Getting accepted by a film festival, any film festival feels great. It means someone "gets" your film. Take a moment to savor this. Sweet. Now what?

1. Thank them. Comply with all their requests regarding transportation, accommodation, materials, etc.

2. Review the screening times and dates they give you. Is your film about seniors? Have they programmed it at 11:30 at night? Probably not, but check right away, while it can still be changed.

3. Put their official festival laurel logos on all of your promo materials right away.

4. Start working on getting people in that city to be interested.

5. Social media your heart out. Sites like Facebook can connect your movie with thousands of like-minded individuals in a given city.

6. Create a postcard to hand out at the event. Print both sides, have screening info, awards, and quotes. Again, why must we see this?

7. Contact the press outlets in that city. What about your film will interest the viewers/readers there? Again, remember how hard it is to interest people. Work it.

8. If you have some special skill (you shot your movie with a cell phone), offer to participate in a forum on something related. Pull your weight.

9. Update your website.

Festivals generally have a party atmosphere. For many of the attendees it is a party. Not for the working director. This is business. Here are a few things I've picked up:

1. Hand out your cards to everyone. Never stop promoting. Take a bunch of 11"x17" handbills. Put them everywhere relevant.

2. Meet filmmakers. Watch their films. This is my favorite kind of film school.

3. Speak before your film — if possible. Audiences almost always enjoy a film by someone they like. Set it up by being likeable. The exception would be if you're the sort who comes off as self-centered. Audiences sniff that out in a heartbeat. Keep the words "I" and "me" to a bare minimum.

4. Notice during the show when people squirm in their seats, go to the bathroom, walk out. This is valuable experience for next time.

5. Encourage people in the Q&A session. Compliment a good question. Comment on the participant's insight. Be polite. Don't brag. Remember it's just a little movie — not a cure for cancer. Be *grateful* people watched it.

6. This one is so important. I almost always forget. Ask audiences to leave online comments at places like IMDb.com. Broadcasters check this. If you have 1,000 positive reviews, that carries weight.

Most importantly, *what's your next project*? Imagine your film really lights up the festival. You'll be the toast of the town. Know what the industry heavies are going to see? A director who can fill seats. Know what they're going to ask you? "What's your next project?"

Going to a festival without a follow-up film to pitch is a badly missed opportunity.

There's something else the industry people at the festival may ask you about. "Do you have distribution?"

This is a loaded question.

[Doing film festival Q&A. Tina Schliessler photo]

chapter five

SELLING YOUR FILM

aking money is nice. But for those bent on becoming a
working director, money is not your primary objective.
Let's restate what your primary objective is:

You want the people who finance films to take you seriously as a director.

It was said earlier that the two ways of doing this are to either make
waves or make money. Usually if you do one, the other will follow,
but it's not necessarily so. Fame is great, but you can make a small
film that doesn't do much at festivals but picks up a good distribution
deal and sells aggressively at MallMart checkouts — which may cause
people to take you quite seriously. So let's talk about the money a bit.

Why not do it yourself? The small film can make a tidy sum in self-
distribution. One can tour for a year or two living off the box office
from well-promoted screenings. Selling DVDs on your website can be
quite lucrative. A filmmaker with a popular film can sometimes make
small TV sales directly at festival markets too. Up until fairly recently
filmmakers could raise a great deal of production financing through
TV pre-sales. And although that market has slowed a lot in the last
while it's still possible if one has a strong idea, perseveres, and is really
lucky. But to do large-scale sales, one often needs the expertise of a
distributor.

DISTRIBUTORS — COUNT YOUR FINGERS AFTER SHAKING HANDS

Problem is, in my and my peers' experience, few of them are honest. I
could buy a waterfront home if the distributors who owe documented
amounts on revenues they've received distributing my films paid

what they clearly owe. For me and their hundreds of other filmmaker victims, it will never happen. They use our money to hire lawyers and accountants to hide behind. You guys know who you are. We were all so sorry to hear your Bentley got keyed, and your plastic-boobed trophy wife cheated with the pool guy while her yappy little purse dog had explosive diarrhea all over the white, silk drapes. Tragic really.

It's kind of hard to be gracious toward those who have actually stolen food out of your kid's mouths.

[Homemade sign, New Orleans, Louisiana. Charles Wilkinson photo]

But, there are distributors who are ethical. The one I'm working with right now, Avi Federgreen of IndieCan, is not only a hard-working distributor, he's fun to work with and invites collaboration on all aspects of the enterprise. How can you know up front? There are tell-tale signs:

1. Are they prepared to *risk* anything? Are they offering you a cash advance against revenue? How hard they'll work for you is directly proportional to how much they're willing to risk.

2. Is there a provision for you to take a piece of the first and every dollar in the door?

3. Is there anything to stop them from taking your work and pocketing all the proceeds?

If the answer to all of the above questions is "no," this is definitely going to end badly.

But a capable distributor can set up a theatrical run. They can facilitate TV sales. They can sell your film into other markets you have no access to — educational, foreign, etc. Please don't get me wrong. An honest and talented distributor is as critical to your success as George Martin was to the Beatles. It's just that at the lower end of the market they're really few and far between.

Worst case scenario is not that they'll just rob you. It's only money, after all. No, worst case is when they're incompetent too — when they don't even get the film out there. This is an easier question than the honesty one. It's easy to research if the distributor chasing you has gotten major play for his other films. If they have, try asking them to show you receipts for payments made to other filmmakers like you. If they have a good record here, take the risk. You never know.

Hold up.

There are times we need to step back and assess where we are, how far we've travelled. This is one of those times. If we're even *talking* about money it means you've made a movie that's making waves. If we're even *talking* about choosing a distributor it means… wait for it…

You're in.

You've made a successful first film. You have a real credit. There are industry people who will take you seriously as a working director now.

Congratulations.

If this were a video game, you've just made it to a whole new level. Cue the cut-scene music.

Here we go!

[In L.A. on the network's dime. Concierge photo]

chapter six

SETTING UP SHOP

Your first film did well, maybe amazingly well. Question is, did it perform so well that you are being offered significant mainstream projects? If so, congratulations. If not, still congratulations — you've made a major first move. You're someone who stands a good chance of getting paid directing work. Now the big question is:

WHERE'S ALL THAT WORK?

Much of this first section will be known and understood by the more established directors. You seasoned directors may want to pretend it's a spec script from your neighbor's best friend and skim.

London, New York, Sydney, Vancouver, Munich, Paris, Montreal, New Orleans, Hong Kong, Bombay, Toronto, Rome, Prague, and more. All cities that produce programming for international exhibition. There are many directors in these centers who work day in, day out. And there are directors who work for a time in these places, then take their credits to Hollywood hoping that the talent they've demonstrated will put them ahead of the crowd. The first task is to find out who's shooting what and where.

How do you find out? There are many ways, some very simple. The Directors Guild of America (DGA) knows where every union show in the U.S. is being shot, as does the International Alliance of Theatrical Stage Employees (IATSE), and the Screen Actor's Guild of America (SAG). They have availability lists, production lists, all kinds of info. They make the info freely available to their thousands of members. And even if you don't have a card, it's not exactly top secret.

In Canada, the Director's Guild of Canada (DGC) maintains offices in all of the major regions. In Britain, BECTU has the info.

What do you need to know?

Where are they shooting the kind of show you're most likely to get hired onto?

Is there a **trend** at work? Is production increasing or decreasing? Why?

Why are they shooting there? Are there local tax breaks? Is it non-union?

Who are they hiring to direct? From where are they hiring them?

Are there **local restrictions** on who can be hired to direct?

LOCAL RESTRICTIONS/PERKS

Some jurisdictions make use of local incentives to attract and stimulate development of a film industry. Often these incentives include some type of point system for the key creative personnel. That's us. Their idea is to encourage the production company to hire as many locals as possible.

It is critical for you to establish if this is a factor in the area where you wish to work. If so, there may be a simple solution. Consider becoming a local. Some directors attempt this as a sort of scam and they're frequently met with resentment. On the other hand, those who approach it by truly becoming a part of the local arts community are frequently welcomed. After all, what community wouldn't want a talented artist as a member?

Even where there's no official residency requirement it can still be an issue. Are one or more shows you feel you're qualified for shooting in New Orleans this season? Are the production companies flying their directors in? Is your aunt's best friend a New Orleans resident? Does she have a spare room? That makes you a local. You just saved the production company airfare and hotels. To a producer who is shooting in New Orleans for economic reasons, that's an incentive.

International co-productions have become a considerable source of quality work. Co-pros always have nationality requirements for their directors. Which rules you out, right? Not necessarily. Was your father born in England or France or Spain or wherever? How about your grandmother? Get in touch with the consulate. Find out what their rules are regarding repatriation and joint citizenship. You never know. Maybe you're entitled to a Euro card. Which is going to increase your chances at being a working director. If you're not a U.S. citizen but wish to be eligible for directing jobs in the U.S., get a green card.

[With the camera crew on *The Highlander*. Charles Wilkinson photo]

GUILD AFFILIATION

All major production centers have union agreements in place. Which for the director means guild membership. A guild card won't get you a job. Nobody gets hired because they have a card. But sometimes not having the right card can impact on your ability to work.

Low-budget shows often fly under the radar. They are seen as a means of breaking in. The guilds and unions tend to look the other way. The higher budget shows in Hollywood simply purchase DGA membership for their first-timer. But for the bulk of the projects, the working director needs to join the appropriate guild.

Generally a DGA card works pretty much everywhere. The reality is that U.S. companies have produced so much work in so many international jurisdictions and have brought so many DGA directors in to do those shows that there are agreements in place almost everywhere for DGA directors.

To work in Canada you need membership in the DGC. In Britain a BEC-TU card does the trick. But the DGA has negotiated reciprocal agreements with these Guilds and few countries will risk driving away lucrative U.S. production by enforcing their labor laws. So a DGA card usually gets you a work permit in Canada or Britain.

Joining the DGA is uncomplicated. You need to be hired to direct by a DGA signatory producer and pay the initiation fees and yearly dues.

The Agent

Do you have the right agent? Should you look for a better one? Do you need an agent at all? Consider this: virtually every director finds and signs their first life-changing deal *without the aid of an agen*t. That first low-budget movie. The first music video that lights the kindling that starts the fire that will become your career. No agent on earth can light that fire for you. Nobody in the directing trade gets "discovered." BUT, once you start a merry little blaze no one can turn it into a roaring bonfire like a good agent. So if your excuse for not working is that you have the wrong agent or no agent at all, that may be just what it is. An excuse.

If you're not currently working, it's because the people doing the hiring aren't thinking about you. Or they're thinking the wrong things about you. Assuming you are qualified for the work, the right agent may be able to change this situation. But how do you get the right agent? By being a promising director. And how do you do that?

Direct. Wherever you can. Do a play that gets good notices. Do a music video for a group about to break out. Do a commercial on spec, a student film, a wedding. Enter every festival under the sun. Win an award. Suddenly the agent sees you (and more importantly can sell you) as the award-winning director who just….

Can The Right Agent Get You Work?

Sometimes. If you are studio or network approvable for the kind of work you want, and if your agent is in that particular loop, then yes, they can. What does that mean?

If you've directed 20 episodes of primetime drama and if your agent talks daily with the producers who hire for primetime drama, then your agent can probably get you more of the same kind of work. Can that agent get you a studio feature? Almost certainly not.

On the other hand, let's say you have one low-budget feature to your credit. Say it didn't go theatrical, but a few critics liked it and it won some awards. Can an agent who's plugged into the world of small features get you serious job interviews for more of the same? Yes. Can that agent get you on to this season's hot primetime episodic? Almost certainly not. Agents specialize.

GM Goodwrench mechanics know nothing about fixing Ferraris. They never see one. Likewise, the perfectionist Ferrari mechanic wouldn't know where to start on that $49.95 tune-up.

Directors often complain about their agents. The agency is too small. Nobody takes their calls. Or they're too big. They don't take *your* calls. Or they're addicted to packaging. They claim your name doesn't have the sizzle that the latest ex-rocker first-timer's does. The complaints may very well be true.

But the complaints we make about our agents are often excuses.

Put yourself in the agent's place. They can't stay in business if they don't have income. In a way, an agent is like a salesman. Give a salesman a desirable product and they'll move it. As anti-art as it sounds, if you make yourself that desirable "product" your agent will sell you.

Big vs. Small

Everybody wants to be rep'd by CAA, ICM, or WME. They rep the biggest of the big. Some of that success is bound to rub off on you, right? And also, their sweatshirts are cool. Who doesn't enjoy a visit to the park with "Property of Wm. Morris Endeavor" on their chest? And their logo on your resume and demo reel. What producer won't put that one at the top of the pile?

Pure fantasy.

I was represented by the Morris Agency for several years. I worked, but not one of my jobs came from them. Why?

Because the kind of lower-level work I was approvable for was simply not going to Morris clients. And of the few jobs my agent there could have sold me for, he had other clients with better credits. When I came to my senses and signed with an L.A. agency that was tops in my field, my phone started to ring again.

Was I wrong to sign with Morris? No. Besides directing, I write spec screenplays. During the time I was there, two or three of my scripts were seriously looked at by people who could have helped them happen if the material was right. That chance, however slim, was worth something.

My point? The big/small criterion isn't the way to choose an agent. So what is?

Here's a way I've found that works. Pick a number of shows you realistically could have been but weren't considered for. Find out who directed them and who represents those directors. Call these agents. Tell them who you are. Ask for a meeting. If you've been truly realistic regarding where you stand a chance of being hired, odds are the agents will want to meet you.

Here's another method that can work very well. Say you've found the agent that's perfect for you. Only problem is they don't want to sign you just now. What to do?

Bring *them* your best lead. Do the agent's job for them. Find a job you are hirable for. Do the leg work. Call for yourself. Take the meeting. Again, if you were correct in your judgment about how hirable you are the producer will talk to you without an agent being involved. Once it looks like they want you, go to the agent and ask them to close and commission what amounts to a done deal. In a way it's a kind of bribery. But it also shows you're motivated. And most importantly it tells the agent that you take responsibility for your own career.

The same applies when you have an agent but you're considering a change. Don't wait until you're into a slow patch to shop around. Who wants to rep an unemployed director? Make the calls when you're working. Very few agents will refuse to meet a working director.

Bottom line, there are *so* many agents out there. Every one of them is right for someone. Get the right one for you.

Speaking of bribery, *reward your agent*. Let them share in your excitement. Every time they get you work buy them flowers or a fruit basket. When they get you work in Paris, send them a print from the Louvre. When they get you work in Germany, say it with *lederhosen*.

THE DEMO REEL

Who needs a reel? This year's Oscar winner doesn't. A director with one show doesn't. Pretty much everyone else does. The first and most important thing to consider is this: who's going to be watching it? The producers of the shows you want to do. The studio people, the network execs, the distributors and their personal assistants. In other words, busy people. They may watch your reel rapidly clicking "next next next" while they're on the phone. Seriously. I've sat in rooms with producers while they watch other director reels like that. You have to bet they do the same with mine and yours.

What's going to make them take their thumb off the next button? For some it will be a famous face or a wild action sequence or a love scene. Others will want to see scenes like the type of show they're producing. Funny scenes for a comedy. Dramatic scenes for a drama. So it's important you send a reel that's appropriate.

Demonstrating the Wrong Stuff

The environment they're watching your demo in is frequently not conducive to quiet reflection. There are tapes and head shots all over the desk, phones ringing, assistants in and out, CNN running full-time on one of the monitors, barely controlled chaos. They've got other director reels to go through. What are some sure-fire turn-offs?

Wrong Genre: "*This is an action director, we're going for comedy.*" Next.

Wrong Craft: "*Oh great, a montage of explosions, grins and kisses cut to the latest pop music. Give them a job as editor.*" Next.

Too Short: "*Is that all they've got? This director lacks experience.*" Next.

Too Long: "*Yeah, uh huh, got it already. What else? Nothing?*" Next.

Old Titles: "*Wow, I used to watch that when I was a kid. That director must be ancient....*" Next.

Poor Quality: "*What? Was that shot on a handycam?*" Next.

All bad.

Demonstrating the Right Stuff

A good reel tells them you can direct.

A good reel tells the people watching it that you can do *their show*. In this age of non-linear editing, every director with a home computer can make multiple versions of their reel.

A good reel is clearly labeled. It has your info and a table of contents on the box as well as on the tape/disc itself. A good reel has good scenes. It tells the viewer that full shows are available on request with a phone number right there.

A good demo reel impresses, wows, entertains. It gets you seriously considered. For what? You've moved to the right town. You've got an agent or you're working up to it. You've got a set of reels for all occasions. What's missing?

FINDING THE JOBS

The most certain route into the director's chair is to get yourself attached to a good script. It's become common for the studios to take on a first-time director if their script is perceived to be hot enough. How do you get attached? Obviously, if you write your own script, you're attached. But screenwriting is a dark art in its own right. Those directors wise enough to realize they can't write can still get attached to a terrific script. There are many unattached screenplays in the world. Thousands of new ones every day. Emerging screenwriters are highly motivated to get their work produced. Most cities have screenwriting groups and workshops. Drop by. Seek out the talent. Develop some relationships. There are thousands of credible producers who will take you on in a heartbeat if you bring them a viable project.

But most working directors are not attached to scripts. They simply get hired to do a job. By whom?

How Do You Find Out About These Jobs?

Most directors look for work most of the time. Even if your agent knows what's out there and has you up for it, that still leaves room for some potential work to fall through the cracks. Your agent may never hear of low-budget projects. And yet there are many such projects you would do well to consider. Who wouldn't have directed *The Blair Witch Project* on spec?

Producers are sometimes very secretive about their plans. Maybe they're in delicate negotiations with a star. Maybe they're having rewrite problems. Maybe they're holding out for union concessions. There are any number of reasons a producer wouldn't announce. Most of an agent's day is occupied trying to run these rumors to the ground. They miss some. That's where you come in.

The second you hear of a real project that you might be right for, call your agent. If you know before they do, they'll be happy you called. Even if they knew, it lets them know you're on the job.

Your Guild office knows the minute a producer starts hiring office PAs. Stay in touch. Make certain they have your updated info. Make the occasional social call to your producer and production manager (PM) friends. Pay attention to the trades, the grapevine.

Less obviously, maintain your contact with the *headwaters*, the high mountain streams that will become raging rivers. Where is *that* at? It's not tough to foretell where the next hot filmmakers are going to come from. The film schools, the 5D underground. Volunteer. Set up screenings of your work, seminars. You as a working director are welcome in these places. Because you've got something they want. Credibility. You're a working director. And they have something you want. An inside track to tomorrow.

To Schmooze Or Not To Schmooze

In my experience, industry parties, festival galas, schmooze fests don't get you work. They can be depressingly shallow celebrity-driven greed/envy lie-a-thons that make you wish you had chosen a career shepherding in the Pyrenees.

They can also be a venue to renew old acquaintances, eat great free food, drink expensive free liquor, and show the community that in spite of all the gossip to the contrary, you're still alive and kicking.

Free food and liquor aside, there is some value in maintaining a presence in the community. And yes it's *possible* someone will mention a project you could be right for. Just not real probable. Three tips: Drink moderately; Don't hit on anyone; Know when to leave.

There's a Job Out There

Ultimately you beat the bushes, go to the parties, read the trades, overhear someone's cell call. You sniff out a job that sounds right. You get your name and material in front of the person who makes the hiring choice. Want to know something amazing? If you keep this up and have just an average amount of luck — they WILL call.

Early on in my career I shamelessly pitched a producer who had a project way over my head. He didn't hire me. Over the years I kept pitching. He kept not hiring. I bumped into him one day, remembered I'd heard he was doing something new, again over my head. I pitched him anyway. Halfway through I stopped, smiled, and said, "*You're never going to hire me, are you.*" He smiled back and said, "*I just did.*"

Congratulations, you've set up shop.

[*The Legend of the Ruby Silver.* Myrl Coulter photo]

chapter seven

THE PHONE RINGS

"Hi, this is _____ calling about a project to see if you would be interested and available. Please get back to me...."

E very single call that comes in sparks a heart rate increase. It should. Some calls mark the beginning of the most wonderful projects. And some not. How do you tell which calls are which?

Your initial objective when answering "The Phone Call" is to establish three key things:

1. Is this project for real?
2. Is the project of interest? Do I want to do it?
3. Am I being offered a job? Or a chance to audition?

WHO'S CALLING?

By considering the source of the call, you can make some assumptions about the potential job and how you should react.

If it's your agent telling you that studio/network/producer XYZ is interested in you for a project, chances are the project is real in the sense that there's a fair probability that the project meets basic industry standards and that you will likely receive an acceptable offer if you respond accordingly.

If the call is coming from a friend, a social acquaintance, or some person/company you've never heard of, it could be a vastly different story and may call for a different response.

One easy shortcut is to field your calls in front of your computer. As soon as they tell you their name, do an IMDb search. A quick Internet search won't tell you who they absolutely are, but it may tell you who they're *not*.

What's The Status Of The Job?

Is it green-lit, "flashing green," in actual development, gasping for life, or one of the thousands of projects circulating around that will never go into production?

If the call comes from your agent they'll say something like, "*It's an HBO mini-series slated for the fall. They want you for three months starting in August.*" There it is. Green-lit. They'll want you to read the script and talk things over. If all that goes well you're as good as hired.

If your agent tells you it's "flashing green," that means the studio or network will green-light it when the producer secures one or more key elements. Usually stars, often a decent re-write, occasionally the director. If they're talking to you at this point it likely means they believe you can assist them to get the green to go solid. You go in, meet their prospective star, pitch your take on the story, help the writer with the script, have lunch with the studio/network people, and away you go. The downside is it's a lot more work, you don't get paid extra for it, and if the show performs poorly, you will take a larger than usual share of the blame. On the upside, you get a project on which you're allowed meaningful input. No contest.

When the call comes from anyone other than your agent, a working producer or a studio/network, some reliable method must be found to establish the current status of the project. Hollywood agents have developed a really subtle way of intuiting what's what with an unknown project. Within the first few seconds of a call they will ask, "*Is this project financed?*" If the answer is, "*Yes, we go to camera in 8 weeks.*" — there it is, green-lit. In other words, you can now move on to focus on content. Do you like it? If the answer is, "*It's a deferral picture. We all believe in the show so much we're doing it for points....*" that's not *necessarily* bad. More and more projects are going on a low- or no-budget basis to try and circumvent the star/studio system. There's nothing intrinsically wrong with doing a good show on spec. It's just important to know up front.

What Are They Actually Saying?

Are they offering you the job, or offering you a job *audition*? Again, if it's your agent and they're talking about dates, you know they intend to hire you unless you choose to pass.

But frequently what's being said (although not in so many big words) is, "*Let's talk. If you impress us, we'll send you a script. If your take on the material impresses us and if the network/studio feels the same, it's yours.*"

It's obviously REALLY important to quickly sense whether you're being offered the job or a chance to audition. If you pitch too hard on a job that's essentially yours, you'll introduce doubt where none previously existed. Conversely, if you don't realize that you're auditioning, you might create the impression that you're not all that interested.

So "The Call" comes in. You talk with them for a while. You learn what the project is — when, where, who. You also intuit how solid the people are. Why they're calling you, what they're actually saying to you, and what your chances are of getting it. If by this point both of you are still talking, chances are you're going to be reading the script.

THE SCRIPT ARRIVES

The script arrives, you sit down to read. What are you looking to find?

By the time you finish your first read of a script you should be able to say, "*Hey, what a good idea for a show.*" If the script, however flawed, is built upon a good strong story, the director has something to work with. But if the story is weak, it doesn't matter what you bring: great dialogue, terrific action, cool shooting and cutting. It won't be enough. This is a tough call to make when you need work. But you need to remember: the only thing worse than a hole on your resume is a horrible credit.

At the same time, it's important to think these things through pretty carefully. When my agent sent me the script for the first *Air Bud*, I said, "*A dog playing basketball? What kid's going to buy into that?*" In retrospect, I made the right choice, but for the wrong reasons.

For now let's assume the script you've been sent falls somewhere between excellent and good.

"Hi, I Read Your Script And...."

Stop!

Remember back in grade school when the cute kid sitting two rows over sent you a Valentine's card — "*Be Mine.*" You know they may have sent the same card to others. Your immediate goal became working up the nerve to pick up the phone and ask them if they'd go to the Valentine dance with you.

Now you've been sent a script. *Be my director.* You have to call them back. Before you pick up the phone, consider what school kids used to (and probably still) do. We'd *rehearse* the phone call for hours before making it. So what are you going to talk about?

"What's Your Take On The Material?"

They want to know if you get it and if you like it and if you think you can do a good job with it. In simple terms, what makes this script special to you? Sometimes, if you've been e-mailed the script, your first reaction could take the form of a short reply e-mail. For example, a while back I responded via e-mail to a script I received in this manner. My initial comment: "*It's a very good story. The script is developing it nicely, making me feel for the characters. This show has potential to be very entertaining.*" The producers responded positively. We moved on to the next level.

The next question you can count on being asked: "*Do you have any script notes?*" Of all the questions a working director must answer, this one is the trickiest. I try and see it from the producer's side. Frequently they've been through development for months already. They've sat through meetings with executives who may have made crippling script demands. Think they want more of the same from me? So... I should just say the script is brilliant and move on, right? Wrong. For two reasons. One small one and one big one. The small one is, most producers are smart people. They know their script isn't perfect. How impressed will they be if I don't notice? The big reason, you get what you settle for. The story may need minor changes as we go along. If I claim it's perfection now, how am I going to do my job?

So in planning the phone call I'll plan to talk about the elements that make the key story points work. In the case of the script I received last night, it's a feature about a woman discovering she was separated at birth from her identical twin. The twin is murdered. She sees the murder in a vivid dream. As a "witness" she becomes a target. There is a lot to like about the story. The central characters are strong and unusual. A murdered twin sister is a powerful inciting incident. The location, New Orleans, is exotic.

One of the notes I planned to make is that the lead character could be a bit more idiosyncratic. A bit more fun. This should remind the producers I'm interested in casting, character, and performance. It will give the producer a chance to jump in and either agree or display a penchant for over-controlling, "*Just not too idiosyncratic, OK?*"

Because I know the script is a first draft I'll plan to try to leave the door open to change. In this particular case my two biggest notes are that whoever the killer is, their overall motivation needs strengthening. Why did they kill the sister in the first place? In this case it was for money, but at present the details are weak. I think that part needs developing. And secondly, given the show is a "whodunit," we need the revelation of the antagonist to be both surprising and inevitable. These are not major structural notes. But presented wrongly, they could get our creative collaboration off to a bad start, or worse yet, no start at all. I think I'm ready now.

THE CALL-BACK

I've read the script, made my notes, booked the call. A few obvious notes. I disable my "call alert" function. It's distracting. I take the call someplace quiet and secure. I have a pitcher of water standing by in case my throat goes dry. I take some deep breaths and punch the numbers. I'm on.

From this point forward I'll relate how it usually goes when I call the producers back. It's speculation, but this is how it usually goes.

They will ask for my take. I'll reiterate my "strong story, lots of potential" comment. They will ask about script changes. I'll feel my way through that.

They will want to talk about cast. They may have one or more lead roles cast as part of the financing. I'll make the call in front of my computer so I can search the actors I don't know. If and when they ask me my opinion, I've got a few ideas I'm happy to share.

Tech Talk

There's a pretty good chance they'll want to get a quick reaction from me on the practical aspects of shooting in New Orleans. *"What do you feel about shooting it in six weeks?"* That sort of thing. I don't know yet what their proposed schedule is. But if they want to shoot this feature in eight days I need to know that right now. Or if they want 16-hour days, 7-day weeks. These are things I need to consider before proceeding further. Obviously some things are outright deal-breakers. No point in wasting anyone's time. But it's good to be patient here. If they ask me if four weeks are do-able, a good answer might be something like, *"Depends. If it's super well organized and you get the right crew and locations…."* Patience.

The call will draw to a close. I'll have a decision to make. Do I want the picture? The producers will have a decision to make. Do they want me? Let's cross our fingers and say the answer to both questions is yes. In the case of the aforementioned New Orleans murder mystery, I can tell you that this particular project didn't go forward — in part due to script deficiencies. The producers replaced it with one intended for a family market about a woman and her two attractive daughters experiencing a home invasion by desperate but inexplicably chaste thugs during a hurricane near New Orleans. In retrospect it should have been obvious that this concept was fundamentally flawed. The show got good ratings, fair reviews, even played a few festivals. But in the end, it *always* boils down to story, and this one came up short.

[With the crew on set in Louisiana on *Heart of the Storm*. Melissa Gilbert photo]

So let's leave that one aside for now and carry on with the process.

THE MEETING

"They want to meet you, it's just a formality" — *What agents say when there's a 50/50 chance you'll get the job.*

"The Meeting" is critical. For the working director, if the meeting goes well there's a high probability you'll be offered the job and you'll accept it. If it goes badly you either won't get an offer, you'll pass, or you'll end up taking a job you know in advance could have problems.

Ideally the first meeting is an opportunity for you and the producer/s to talk informally. To get a sense of each other. To get a feeling of how your and their approach to the project would mesh. *"Do we agree on the material, can we get along?"*

Directing Yourself in The Meeting

By now you've had a chance to analyze "The Call-Back." You've reflected on how the producer responded to your pitch. You know that they responded well to a particular set of ideas you had. You know they responded less well to other ideas.

You've had a chance to study the script with this new knowledge. You sense where they want to go with the project. You may have some new script ideas. Possible solutions to problems identified during that conversation.

You have studied the characters. You've gained insights into them. It's always good to refer to the characters by their cast names. It shows you know the script.

You have some ideas about cast. It's often worthwhile to refer to a role as Meryl Streep-*like* or Brad Pitt-*like*. The humor is always appreciated (think we can get him/her?) and it's a kind of shorthand.

You will also have formed some ideas about crew. One big discussion point will be the director of photography. Have some viable suggestions. Be careful about proposing film school friends unless they have the solid credits to back it up.

You may have ideas about locations. If you are a local, here's your chance to show how well you know the area.

You will have formed some ideas about the style the picture should have. You will have opinions about lens choice, camera mode (handheld, etc.).

You have given thought to schedule issues: "*Three weeks in the city location, two weeks at the beach location, one week on a stage.*" That sort of thing. Rough scheduling will also clue you in as to where the producer's coming from. If it's a 4-week TV movie with a lot of action sequences at sea during a storm, it's pretty obvious you're shooting in a wave pool with a significant 2nd Unit out chasing weather. If it's an inexperienced producer who wants to do it all on location with 1st Unit, be afraid. Be very afraid.

The Objective

Prior to going into the meeting you need to be clear with yourself about your own goal. If you want the picture no matter what, then that's your goal. Meet, shake hands, pitch, hope for the offer.

But often your goal will be dependent upon the producer's goal. Obviously if you get a sense that the producer's goal is to tuck a few hundred thousand into his jeans and let you take the rap from the critics, your goal becomes getting his assistant to validate your parking and getting gone. Alternatively if his goal is winning an Oscar or an Emmy, what a happy coincidence. Wouldn't it be great if you knew in advance what the producer's goal is? You can.

IMDb search all the producers. If they have a resume chock full of quality projects, chances are they'll probably want quality this time as well. My take on this is that there are four categories of producer. Award Winners, Solid Quality, Emerging, and Sleaze. Award Winner speaks for itself. You've heard of them or their shows. They have awards. Solid Quality is much more common. These are the vast majority of producers who produce the vast majority of quality shows. They generally pay their bills and keep their words. The Emerging producer is a tough call. All you can do is find out who else is part of their team, who's financing, and what the script is like. Sleaze is easy to spot. Their credits often start in the '70s with quasi porn/ action titles, through the '80s it's bad action adventure that went straight to tape, in the '90s they jumped on the "family fare" bandwagon. In the new century they're scrambling for what they can get. Beware.

Follow the money. Find out who is financing the show. Is it a studio, one of the big networks, a small specialized network? Or is it mysterious "foreign money," an "investment syndicate," a known house of schlock?

If the money is coming from a reputable source, it's no guarantee that the show will be good. But it should guarantee a minimum standard of behavior and quality. If the money is coming from a questionable source, your odds are not good.

Pre-judging based on past behavior isn't always fair. And it's not always 100% accurate. But things add up. If the script is borderline bad, if the money is sleazy, if the producer has a history of dreck, you know where you stand.

What Are They Thinking About You?

Remember: they have IMDb too. They have telephones. They're bound to know some of the people you've worked for. They may have seen your work and read your reviews. They're going to have formed an opinion of you too. What is that opinion likely to be?

Play the devil's advocate for a sec. Put yourself in the producer's chair. Research *yourself*. Go over your resume. What kind of picture emerges? What would a stranger intuit to be your strengths and weaknesses? Play devil's advocate. Make the accusations. You're not experienced enough. You're too young or too old. You've never done comedy, or drama, or visual effects. You've never worked with a difficult star. You've been idle for a while — Drugs? Alcohol? You've never done an action show or a kid's show. Why aren't you famous?

When you walk into the meeting they're going to be looking at you from *that* point of view, regardless of how true and accurate that picture of you actually is. You need to be able to speak to that.

[With actor Gary Chalk, Will Waring, and David Geddes. Tina Schliessler photo]

Come In

The assistant shows you in. Hands are shaken. First looks are exchanged. Have a seat. Want something to drink? They may say some nice things about you. Be ready to reciprocate. What show/s have they done that you admire? Praising them is not necessarily sucking up. You know the incredible hurdles *you've* jumped to be able to sit here in this room on this day and call yourself a director. The producer's feat is no less amazing. Respect the achievement.

Be prepared to have a conversation lasting anywhere from ten minutes to a few hours. When the producer talks, don't just catch your breath. LISTEN. Nine times out of ten what they're trying to tell you is *how to get the job*.

There will be times when you'll be in a meeting and you'll realize this job is just not for you. But recognizing that this job is wrong for you doesn't mean your work is done here. You need to let them down easy. A little diplomacy is worth a lot. This particular project may not be your cup of tea, but who's to say their next one won't be? A politically savvy Hollywood producer once told me:

"Everyone who isn't your friend... is your enemy."

Jeez, that's an encouraging thought.

There will also be times when you really want the job but sense the meeting is going badly. It's often not that hard to intuit. Sometimes when I sense it's going against me, I'll say something like:

"Almost everything I've ever directed is still in regular exhibition. I'm a good director. I relate very well to the actors. I get good performances. I motivate the crew to work quickly and well. I come prepared. I shoot efficiently. I rarely need overtime. I compose interesting shots that are also cut-able as coverage. I tell the story and my shows always play well. If I do your show, it may be we'll get along and want to work together again. I have many repeat credits. It may be we won't hit it off. But the bottom line is, I'll direct an entertaining show that makes us all look good."

This approach has gotten me quite a lot of work, because it's the truth.

Regardless of how well the meeting goes, it's unusual to receive an offer on the spot. That can take days, sometimes weeks. Even longer. I try to think about something else. One meeting, they promised to call back within the hour. They didn't. I got tired of looking at the phone. I used the time to learn "Blackbird" on the guitar. I finally made it through without a mistake. As the last notes were dying away the phone rang. (I got the job, did my best, show was OK, money's been spent, I still play "Blackbird" around the campfire — happy end.)

THE OFFER

"They called with dates." — The second coolest thing you'll ever hear your agent say.

An offer. Wow!

The manner in which the offer is made depends on the type of show it is. If it's a feature or network long-form, the offer will be negotiated back and forth between your agent and the studio/network. If the offer is for an episode on a series, again it will most likely be your agent doing the talking.

On a low-budget show where you are being asked to do the show for considerably less than guild scale, frequently the offer will be made directly to you. Even if you have an agent. It will be up to you to deal with it initially. But if you do have an agent you may want to consider having them negotiate the final details. More on that later.

On a "no budget" or spec show, where you are being asked to do the show for no money, you'll be doing most of the work the agent normally does. And again, it's worthwhile to get your agent to negotiate the final deal. The principle here is that low- and no-budget shows have a high mortality rate. If you waste a lot of your agent's time chasing down work they ultimately never get paid for, they're going to stop taking your calls.

Regardless of the type of show, the complexity of your negotiation is going to be a function of money. The more money involved, the more negotiating.

"The Bigs." On a studio feature or a network long-form, there's a high probability you won't be working for "scale" (the guild negotiated minimum pay for a show of that type). Most directors who work at the upper end of the business — aka "The Bigs" — are paid "over scale." How much over is a function of your past success and/or how much they want you. There's also an element of poker playing your agent and the producer will engage in. And let's be clear. This is agent country.

Besides your actual fee there's your final credit, your billing on posters and TV ads, your edit rights, your office (how luxurious), your trailer (how long), whether you get a driver or not, how and when you get your dailies, what kind of and how many final copies of the finished show you get, etc, etc. On top of all this, if it's a location show, there are the potentially complex issues of accommodation, *per diem*, travel, travel tickets for your family, what kind of rental car, and on and on.

Sometimes the offer deals with these issues on a "favored nations" basis. In other words, nobody on the show gets better treatment than you. But even then there may be some wiggle room. Let your agent be the bad guy. Just tell them what you need from the deal. As far as the money is concerned, your agent needs to hear from you something like one of the following: "*I want this picture. Make the best deal you can, but don't blow it.*" Or, "*I'm lukewarm about this show. If they don't come up with the right money, pass.*" That type of thing.

When it comes to the details, improperly negotiated small things can become big very quickly. If the shoot is way over on the other side of the city, two hours of self-driving every day is going to get old very quickly. Given how tired you're going to be in the later weeks, it could also be dangerous. Ask that they negotiate a driver. While you're at it, get your agent to negotiate a device that will allow you to watch dailies on the ride home. It's in the production's interest that you get enough rest.

If the show is in Thailand and you need to fly there four times in prep and make several trips home during the shoot, your agent should negotiate first-class airline tickets. Ten hours of cramped, crying baby, tourist-class hell is not going to deliver you to set in any condition to work.

On a long location shoot, accommodations are critical. A fleabag motel is OK for a night or two. So is a tent. But after two months of shooting, you don't need external sources of stress. My general rule is that location accommodations should be of the same caliber as my home. I don't live in palatial splendor. I don't live in a dumpster. But I do live someplace interesting with a good kitchen. On a long shoot, I need that.

Are they giving you a car? We're long past the time when it's anything but irresponsible to drive a gas guzzler. Get an electric or a hybrid. Period.

Need a phone? How about a computer? A bicycle? A health club membership? Video rentals? Tell your agent. But keep in mind that if your demands become excessive, there are directors out there of comparable level who'd do the job for scale.

Episodic

Virtually everything that applies to big-project contract negotiation doesn't apply to episodic. There's very little to negotiate. Typically every director is paid scale. If the show is on location, your agent may get a few extra dollars for *per diem*, maybe a slightly better car. Maybe you can get a digital master at the end. The watchwords with episodic are favored nations. If they give you a Porsche, they have to give all the other directors a Porsche.

With episodic, most of the negotiation is over schedule. You're busy in August and October. Can you do two shows back to back in September? That's what your agent is talking to them about.

Low-Budget

There will be good shows you are offered that simply don't have the money to pay anything near the guild rate. But because of the script or the people, you'll want to do the show anyway. Does that mean no negotiation? Not at all. There are things they can give you instead of money. Like some form of producer credit. Like a piece of the back end, a percentage of the money the producer receives (Warren Beatty was given 40% of gross instead of fees on *Bonnie & Clyde* because the studio wasn't confident. It grossed $70 million…). These things can often be difficult to negotiate. You're frequently dealing with inexperienced producers. Once you've agreed in principle to do the show, it's a good idea to have your agent take it from here.

How Low Can You Go?

Occasionally you'll get an offer that seems offensive. Is it? Do they not have the money, or is the producer trying to chisel you? If you really like the project and need the work, consider taking it on a "no quote" basis. In other words, when the next producer calls your agent and asks what you last worked for, they can't divulge.

Established Players Working On Spec

It is becoming more common even for established producers and actors to do shows (what are called "passion projects") speculatively, with very little cash financing. The promise is made that when the picture goes into distribution, the cast and crew will be paid from the revenue the film earns. In theory it sounds great.

In practice how it tends to work is, a distributor or network will advance money to the producers in return for the right to exhibit the finished show. When audiences start paying to see the finished show, the distributors first subtract their sales commission, 30–40% of every dollar. Then they subtract all the expenses: prints and ads, publicity, travel, hotel, etc. Then they subtract the amount they originally advanced. The net result is that unless the picture is a runaway hit like micro-budget *Defcon 2012*, the distribution expenses and fees tend to gobble up everything. Very few workers on a spec film ever see any money.

There is one way a spec film can guarantee money back to the people who make the film. It's like an ancient whaling expedition where the third harpooner was promised a 265th share in the catch. They'd whale for no wages. Then when the ship docked the blubber and oil would be sold before anyone disembarked. Each sailor would receive cash on the barrelhead.

How that translates into modern film terms is, the producer negotiates the distribution deal such that a *specified percentage of the <u>very first dollar</u> earned from every sale and/or rental is paid to the producer. And a specified percentage of that is paid to you.* Sign a deal like this and you *will* see money.

If the distribution deal is "tiered," that is if anybody gets paid any money before you, chances are you will never see a penny. Got that? You get a piece of the very first dollar? You'll see money. You don't? You're probably working for love.

The Best Possible Deal

Don't let the negotiating spiral out of control. These people are negotiating for and about <u>you</u>. It's your thing. Don't let them harm you and your career by getting into the pissing contests agents, producers, and lawyers sometimes do. Remember that production was delayed for weeks on *The Last Temptation of Christ* because the lawyers couldn't agree on the sequel rights....

YOU GOT THE JOB!

"You got the job!" — The first coolest thing you'll ever hear your agent say.

Seize this moment. Celebrate it. You have just accomplished something that presidents, popes, rocks stars dream of. *You've been hired to direct.*

The moment is perfection. It could easily be one of the key events of your life. It may be your first job. It may be your last. So savor this moment. Because you're about to enter a whole new ball game. You're about to commence the phase of production that dictates how *all* else will go. This set of tasks will set you and the show up for possible success if you do them well, but almost certain failure if you don't. I speak of pre-production. Prep.

[On *Heart of the Storm* in Louisiana. Mark Mervis photo]

chapter eight

PRE-PRODUCTION

"Be prepared." — Boy Scouts of America motto

Virtually every single decision regarding the resources you're going to have to tell this story is made during prep. Technically, prep begins when a project is "green-lit" (green as in *money* flows) and ends on the first day of principal photography. For the working director however, prep begins before prep begins.

TOOLS OF THE TRADE

It's worth mentioning at this point that there are some tools you're going to need.

Besides the computer you need in your home and office, a palmtop with fast wireless Internet is extremely useful.

A cell phone is indispensable. I do all of my studio/network calls hands-free from the car riding to and from set. So when I get home at night I get an extra hour or so of R&R.

A good camera in your phone is invaluable for pitching locations or props to distant producers. It also helps you communicate with your crew during prep.

A GPS unit can be handy for finding set. A satellite phone works great on mountaintops. There's talk of heads-up displays on one's contact lenses....

Things You'll Need In Prep

I toss a big old sports bag in my trunk before driving to the production office every day during prep and then take it to set once we're shooting. Everyone has a different list of contents. Here's mine.

~ A director's viewfinder. An actual steel and glass optical device. Mine is small. It telescopes into lens sizes and has inserts for various aspect ratios.

[Director's viewfinder. Tina Schliessler photo]

~ Rain gear including boots. I buy the best I can afford.

~ In winter, warm gear including silk long underwear, polar fleece vests, hand and feet warmers, and boots. Again, quality is critical.

~ A hat is a must for sun and rain.

~ Sunglasses. I use expensive polarized ones. I frequently twist them around to judge if a polarizing filter would get rid of a particular reflection.

~ A pad, pen, water, a hundred dollar bill, antacid pills, painkillers, a hairbrush, a small first-aid kit, a Frisbee. You'll find yourself in the weirdest situations. It's best to be prepared for anything.

By now it must be fairly obvious that film crew people tend to be gadget people. Some of it you need, some is nice, some is silly. You can waste a lot of time fooling with tech. The whole concept is to save your very limited time.

The Production Office

If you're working for a studio, you'll pull up at the gates, clear security, park and enter. If your show is an independent, you'll pull up at a grungy-looking warehouse with a commercial real estate sign out front. Yes, this is the place. Independent productions rarely waste money on fancy digs. The choice of production office is driven by available space, cheapness of rent, proximity to shooting locations, issues of traffic, crew commute, and so forth.

Follow the signs. Enter the main office. Usually there are two or three workers in the center of a hub of offices. You can expect that the office doors close by will be the producer's, the PM's, the production coordinator's, perhaps the writer's, certainly accounting, and yours. The crafts are usually housed closer to the work spaces. The assistant directors (ADs), the art department, costumes, transportation, and various others depending on the show. There will be a central boardroom for all the meetings. And washrooms and a kitchen/craft service area.

The three or so desk workers are usually very pleasant. They are office production assistants (PAs), maybe an assistant coordinator, possibly an assistant to the producer (who always likes to know who's phoning, who's stopping by). It's their job to run the phones, copy the scripts, distribute the enormous volume of office memos, schedules, etc. Be nice to the office staff. They work long hours for not great pay. Make them know they're a valued part of your team and you'll be surprised how much they will help you.

And This Will Be Your Office....

Your own personal office needs to be big enough to comfortably seat 4-6 people for all the meetings you'll hold here. You'll need a desk, chairs, a phone, a computer w/Internet access, a small printer, and various office supplies. Your office should be private, not shared, with a closable door. But don't be too fussy. You won't spend all that much time here.

So you're in your office. You straighten your pens. What next?

First Things First

Your first real order of business is to take the pulse of the place. Is everything good? Is there trouble? Who is the office heavy? Where are the land mines? You need to find someone who knows the ropes, what's what, who's who, what's in the wind. Keep in mind that there is almost always something going on that you should know about. Maybe one of the distributors is fighting with the producer over a certain key cast member. Maybe you're about to unwittingly weigh in on the opposite side from a person you're going to have to work closely with. Find out what's moving under the surface and don't start out on the wrong side of it. In episodic TV the person you'll get the skinny from is almost always your 1st AD. On long-forms your guide may be the producer, maybe the coordinator, maybe (but less often) the PM. If at all possible you should make this your first real meeting. Your question to them: "*So, is there anything going on I should know about?*"

One note of caution: Everyone on a show has their own canoe to paddle. Make certain that the picture your guide is painting is not simply their paranoid view of what you would otherwise find to be a trouble-free world.

Natural Friends: There are people in the production office who will find it very much in their interest to get along with you. Principally the director of photography (DP), the designer, your assistant directors (ADs), and most of the keys. Their job is just so much more difficult if you don't share a consensus. Which is not to say that all of these people don't have their own agendas as well. But more on that in a minute.

Natural Enemies: The Godfather, Don Corleone, tells his son Michael that the one who will betray him will be the one who asks him for a meeting after the Don's death. When you're prepping a movie, if trouble is going to start at this stage the director's very own Clemenza or Tessio will either be the line producer/ production manager (PM), or the writer. Why? It's simple. The line producer and the PM are there to deliver the show on (or below) budget. You are there to deliver a great show. Occasionally those two aims can clash. The writer fears you are going to change her words and destroy her vision (*often — a vision she's certain would have been expressed beautifully if only she'd been chosen to direct*).

Which is not to say there aren't a lot of line producers, PMs, and writers who are mature, honest filmmakers you'll love working with. But this is where the threat seems to come from most often.

There's a simple way to recognize whether these people are enemies or not. It's in how they come at you: straight or manipulative. Straight is when you say: "*I need five helicopter days.*" And they say: "*Gee, we only have budget for three. But there may be some fat in locations. Let's see if we can work it out.*" If they're prepared to be straight with you they are not your enemy at all.

But sometimes when you say, "*I need five helicopter days....*" They say, "*WHAT???!! Are you crazy!? I got budget for a Cessna 172 for half a day, tops!*" They expect you to scream back and ultimately settle for three helicopter days. Because they're certain that's what you really wanted all along.

You need to figure this one out right away. If you are straight with someone like this, they'll misinterpret that as your (weak) opening negotiating position and they'll proceed to take away stuff you really need to make the picture. And if you then stick to your guns (thus denying them the opportunity to "beat you down") they'll tell the world you're difficult.

Writers can be like that too. Most are straight. They love writing and problem solving. They know you'll find ways of getting their story to translate from their page to your screen. But some writers have been abused so badly that they take up an extreme defensive position right out of the gate. I recently worked with a writer who adopted this "strategy." In one of our early story conferences I had quite a number of very minor notes. Small dialogue things mostly. I also had five more substantial notes. Things like, "*There's a logical conflict if this character knows something they haven't found out yet.*" That sort of thing. The writer fought tooth and nail over every single minor point. No matter how trivial. When it came to the five more important notes he flat out refused to consider changing anything. When I said something about his inflexibility, he screamed at me, "*I gave you 12 out of 20 on your list! Who's being inflexible?!*" That was our last conversation. I got the changes I needed from the producer. Life (and prep) is too short.

THE CONCEPT MEETING

One of your first scheduled meetings will be what is often referred to as the "Concept Meeting." It is here where you will meet the other department heads (keys) already on the payroll. This is where you will have your first chance to begin to communicate your ideas to some of the people who will help you realize them. It gives the beginnings of your crew their first chance to get a sense of your vision. Which is one of the reasons why your first "who's doing what to whom" meeting is so important. If your vision includes that fleet of helicopters, the Concept Meeting is an embarrassingly public place to discover that the PM claims to have budget for just one Cessna.

The Concept Meeting sets the early priorities. What you can and should expect to come out of it are decisions like, "*We need to find a location that works for both the castle and the pool hall.*" Or, "*We need to plan on building the castle interiors on the stage.*" Very general big-picture stuff.

The Concept Meeting is also your chance to demonstrate your tone. They're watching you. They want to know if you're professional, a terminal nice guy, a pushover, a fighter. You are watching the crowd for signs of same.

Meet the Keys

Next will be a series of meetings with the key department heads as they come on board. IMDb search *everyone*. Find something you admire in their work and be ready to praise it when you meet them. This sounds phony. And if you're telling them lies about shows you haven't seen, then yes, it is phony. "*You did props on* John Carter? *That must have been really challenging.*" That's not phony.

In the keys meetings, whether it's for picture cars, makeup, wardrobe, or whatever, the pattern rarely varies. These people have read the script. They have ideas of what their approach should be. They troop into your office with their scripts full of Post-Its and highlighter marks. What they are looking for is direction from you regarding the elements their department will deliver to you. In absence of clear ideas from you they want confirmation that *their* ideas are in sync with your vision.

Invariably your opinions and theirs will differ from time to time. That's OK. It's normal. It's not that you differ that's important, it's how you go about it. Done well it can become a rewarding collaboration. Done badly there's a risk they'll dig in their heels.

Take Wardrobe. The costumer has ideas. She'll have magazine cut-outs and perhaps sketches. When she pitches you her ideas she's revealing something personal to you: her taste. Think about it. When your spouse/partner asks your opinion of one of their outfits, do you say, "*Nah, looks like crap. What else you got?*" Your spouse/partner may not react well to this. Neither will the costumer. She may take it. She may suffer in silence. You're the director. But she'll find a way to make you pay for your rudeness. She will. How hard would it be to say, "*I see where you're going. Interesting. That makes me wonder if perhaps we should consider something a little more like....*"?

This is another place you'll need your "handle" on the script. The one you found back when you were first in discussions with the producer. Keys love shorthand. Like you, they're busy. If you can tell your DP you were thinking of going with something a bit like a show he knows (or will be able to rent), you're miles ahead. One thing your keys do not want to see is signs of over-controlling. The make-up people are looking for general comments about degrees and color. Not what brand of base to use.

But at the end of the day it's your choice. And sometimes the disagreement you find yourself in with a key is not about content. It's not about budget. It's not about style. It's about *control*. Don't cave in to an overbearing department head. Unchecked, they have the ability to ruin your show.

I Really Want to Direct....

Never forget. Many of these people want your job. They think the director gets money, prestige, and power. They often have no clear sense of how hard you had to work to get here. Or how hard you have to work to stay here. Why not? Because they've been too busy working week in, week out, bringing home a steady paycheck at their less competitive craft. They never see the years of sacrifice a struggling director makes turning down paying work as a camera or lamp operator.

But it's hard not to sympathize with the key who wants your job. They sometimes see people handed the director's job based on their achievements as a rock star, DP, producer, nephew. These people are often given directing work without acquiring the skills. Crews are sometimes forced to carry an incompetent or otherwise irrelevant director. The crew people *know* they could direct better. It's a frequent topic of conversation in the lunch line.

Which is why you need to convince them that a) you have earned your job; b) you will pull your weight; and c) *it is more in their self-interest to work <u>with</u> you.* Make them believe in your talent. Make them realize that you'll be working a lot in the years to come. That you're someone who'll be in a position to hire them in the future. Who doesn't want to work with competent people they like and trust?

With A Little Help From My Friends

It's great to hire as many of "your people" as possible for obvious reasons. Generally (although not in episodic) you'll have the most say in the hiring of the DP and your 1st AD. Because they're the ones you work closest with. But there's no reason you can't put forward your other friends. It is an absolute joy to build up over time a group of people you love to work with. If someone is capable, honest, enthusiastic, and on your wavelength, it's a real find. And in all honesty most of the people you work with will be this way. The majority of people who work in our business do so because they love it. They love being good at what they do.

THE ASSISTANT DIRECTOR

During prep there's one department you will be working with more than any of the others. The *directing* department. The assistant directors. The ADs.

The ADs calculate what elements the director is going to need to tell the story and when they're going to need them. Need actors? The ADs organize their pick-up. They monitor their progress through hair/make-up/wardrobe. They deliver them to set just as the director is ready for them. Need a second unit to shoot sunsets from a downtown skyscraper? The ADs schedule it. They put it on the call sheet. It's done.

It's easy to see why the ADs are often considered to be part of the line producer/PM's team. They live where the rubber meets the road. If an AD department works well, things go smoothly. If not, the most minor AD mistake can cost a production thousands of dollars. PMs and ADs maintain a constant dialogue.

From your POV the assistant director is there for one primary thing. To provide what you need to tell the story. There is sometimes also a sense of mentorship. Many of the people who work as assistant directors hope to one day move into the director position. The concept is that by observing closely they'll acquire the tools of the trade. It's been my observation that the more an AD enjoys the filmmaking process the more they'll resist the pull to side with the line producer. And the more likely that AD will make the transition into directing. Conversely the more business-oriented an AD is, the more likely they'll transition into line producing.

Directing The Schedule

During prep all the work the ADs do becomes formalized into one document: the schedule. From the schedule flows everything: the actor's bookings, special equipment needs, call times, shooting order, everything. The schedule dictates what order you will do things in and what resources you'll have to do them. In prep a smart director is all over the schedule like a tourist at a Vegas buffet.

From the outset it's good to discuss the schedule with the AD in general terms to see that you're on the same page. Comments like, "*OK, looks like one week in the mountains, two weeks on the main farm, a week on the stage, and a week of second unit. Sound about right?*" Because if you're shooting what you believe to be an action picture and you get handed a schedule with three weeks of studio dialogue and one week of action… you're not shooting an action picture.

What influence can you have on the schedule during prep? Lots.

Want to shoot sequentially (scene 45 before 46)? In many cases it's possible to schedule at least the scenes you shoot on any given day more or less sequentially. Your cast will love you for it and you'll get better performances. Let your AD know and work the schedule with them.

You visit the location and realize the best sunlight position there is in the morning? Work the schedule.

Want to give your cast an early wrap? A long weekend? Work the schedule.

You and your 1st AD can work together like partners. The big thing is communication. Let your AD know what you need. I always give them my general schedule notes right away. I'll tell them I need X amount of time alone in the locations. Usually weekends. I'll want to meet with all the actors prior to the read-through (usually a drink at night). I'll want to shoot sequentially wherever possible. On night shoots I'll want to schedule the heavy stuff before lunch (we get sleepy after eating), and so on. In other words, I let the AD know how to schedule me.

But Sometimes….

There will be the odd occasion when you end up with a 1st AD whose personal style conflicts with yours. On a long-form show, if you can't fix it really fast in prep, talk to the producer. You can live with an unpleasant lamp operator. But you have to spend all day every day with the AD. See about replacing them.

Obviously in episodic TV, unless the AD goes insane and starts coming to work naked, they're not going to be replaced, regardless of how much you may dislike them. So deal with it. Direct them. Be professional. Do your job competently. Don't make dumb mistakes. Maybe even catch the AD in a few errors. Make them stay on their toes. Worst case you'll end up with a professional relationship. And just maybe… sooner or later the AD will realize you're not the enemy.

[With AD James Marshall and DP Tobias Schliessler on *Max*.
Kharen Hill photo]

Prepping the Script

Prep is your last real chance to deal with the script as a whole. Once shooting starts you'll be focused on acts, scenes, lines, shots.

Does prepping the script mean changing the script? To one degree or another, yes. And know this: arguments over changing the script are the number one cause of director/producer friction during prep. To begin with, what exactly is the director's responsibility to the script during prep?

The director's duty to the screenplay during prep is to make every reasonable effort to ensure that the final shooting script you take before the camera will empower the writer's key ideas to flow smoothly from page to stage such that the best possible film is made.

Prepping the script is polishing off any rough edges that could impede the translation from the writer's written word to the screen. Because that is exactly what the director does with the screenplay — *translate*.

The way a language translator works is to first understand the meaning of the work in the original language. Then they find the ideas/images/words that will express that meaning in the target language. If an American character says, "*I want a hot dog....*" and if the translator translates word for word into French, the result is "*Je veux un chien chaud.*" Literally "*I want a canine at high temperature.*" In short, gibberish.

Judgment is required during every translation process. That's why computerized translation programs don't work very well. That's why producers hire directors. Otherwise they'd save the salary and get the writer to oversee things. Smart producers working with competent directors know that there are judgment calls in the director's handling of the script.

What's on the Table?

The kinds of changes I frequently ask for in prep have to do with things like awkward dialogue. Or I'll ask for a scene's location to be moved to an exterior if we've found a great location. Or I'll question the logic of what and when a character knows.

What shouldn't you be asking for? Well… if it's a biopic about the life of Mother Theresa, prep is not the place to be arguing for a car chase. You should have raised an issue this fundamental in your first meeting with the producer. At that time you may have been less critical when you were trying to land the job than you are now, when you're faced with actually doing the job. If so, this is where you'll have to deal with the consequences. How to proceed in these shark-infested waters?

Re-Re-Read the Script

As many times in as many ways as you can. Read it considering *time passage.* Frequently you'll find that one day seems impossibly long and you'll want to consider putting a night in between. This is usually the result of a lot of scene juggling by the writer.

Read the script from each character's point of view. Sometimes, one character winds up with someone else's lines. Another computer editing glitch.

Read looking for legitimate prep issues. Things that need to be changed because of changes that have arisen in prep. You've cast a formerly male role with a female actor? You may need dialogue changes. You've decided to shoot a scene interior instead of exterior? The script needs to say that or the various departments won't know.

Read looking for any logic gaps. Places where you suddenly see things that don't make sense. Characters who know things they couldn't possibly know. Or who act as though they've seen or heard something we know they haven't. Like the "too long day" syndrome, these types of mistakes frequently occur as a result of the extensive cutting and pasting writers often do.

Read looking for dialogue inconsistencies and just plain awkward or uncommunicative lines. If you don't, your actors will. And remind your producer that it's way less expensive re-writing dialogue during prep than on set.

Read looking for weak or missing devices. The easiest way to sniff out an ineffective device is to look for scenes that are in and of themselves not very entertaining but are there to establish this or that important fact for later on. A good device shouldn't need to be propped up by bad ones. Challenge the writer to find a more direct way.

Big List Small List

Got your list? Cut it in two: 1) things you can shoot around or otherwise deal with yourself; and 2) things that must be addressed by the writer/producer. Because you need to consider how large a problem you're about to become. The total size of your list is critical. Walk into this conversation with a long list, even if most of your points are trivial things caused by casting and location issues and there's a real danger you'll get a percentage of what you need and then they'll start digging in.

With each point ask yourself: do I need this changed in the script? Or can I, as the director, deal with it in shooting? Anything you can shoot around or cut around, don't bother them with it.

Of the things you can't do yourself, logic gaps are fairly easy to raise. Usually a writer will see the light. Time problems, ditto. Dialogue is tougher. If they resist you have to accept that you'll find some way of making the actor say it. But you can always plan to shoot with lots of coverage so you can remove the offensive dialogue in your cut.

Weak devices are sometimes real sticking points. A writer will live with these things so long that they forget what they're for. If the writer/producer resists, ask yourself if you can shoot it to make it clear. If not, here's a place you may need to stand and fight. Remember, if the script is asking you to shoot uninteresting scenes just to prop up an important point, then the device isn't working.

Having separated the things you as the director can fix from the things you need help with, it's time to cut your "need help" list in two again. Cut it into simple stuff and bigger stuff. Take both lists into the writer/producer meeting. Start small. See how it goes. If your minor ideas are met with professionalism, graduate to larger ones. If you meet "over my dead body" kind of resistance, either forget about your major list, or reconsider the style of your approach.

Earn The Right To Change

A director has to *earn* the trust of the writer and producer. That trust doesn't come automatically with signing a deal memo. Ask yourself, if I were Martin Scorsese, would they listen to my script notes? In a heartbeat they would. So maybe the problem isn't your ideas. Maybe it's you. It's the old adage: "If you're so smart, how come you ain't famous?" That's hard to argue with. By all means, give the producer the chance to look at your ideas. But if you aren't famous, what makes your judgment better than theirs? Bottom line — they own the project. They hired you. If they're telling you the script is finished prepping… the script is finished prepping.

What's next? On all shows except ones shot entirely on a stage, it's time to get into the van.

THE LOCATION SCOUT

Everyone knows that most films and TV shows shoot at a combination of specially built sets in a studio, and out on locations. "Location" is any place where filming takes place away from the studio or sound stage. A house, a stadium, an airport, whatever.

The primary challenge with location scouting is to find as many excellent locations as possible at as few actual venues as possible. The goal being *to have the least number of unit moves.* Whether your production unit is a few cars or dozens of giant production trucks, moving is time-consuming and expensive. If you can shoot in one location for at least an entire day the transport folks can move during the night. Even then their overtime is expensive and your crew takes time settling into every new location. As the director, time spent moving is *lost time.* Lost time translates into lost shots, lost set-ups, lost chances for brilliant performances.

There is also the cost consideration. Some locations are outrageously expensive. Some are free. Some cost a lot to control traffic or pedestrians. Some are empty. Some you can drive to. Some you can't even chopper in. All these factors impact on the budget and the schedule.

Location selection and planning takes up a big chunk of prep. The shooting schedule you and the ADs are working on is very much dependent upon which scene will be shot at what location. Say your script calls for a mansion location as well as fields, a swimming pool, and a garage. If you find a country manor location that has excellent sites for all of these things, you will obviously schedule the shooting of the mansion scenes back to back with the fields, pool, and garage scenes. If, on the other hand, the manor has no pool and the only suitable one is miles away, you will schedule that for a different day. Maybe even a different week. Which is going to have an impact on the dates you schedule your actors for. Which could have an impact on one or more actor's availability. It's all interconnected. So the sooner you get a range of excellent choices for your locations, the sooner your schedule will start becoming real.

The way the process will begin is this: after the concept meeting the AD will schedule a meeting between you and the Location Manager (LM) who will by now have a sense of what you're looking for. The LM will have pulled or created a series of file folders full of photos of more or less appropriate locations. Your interest will be aroused to a greater or lesser degree. You'll need a closer look. The AD will schedule a location scout.

Does the working director need to prep for a location scout? Very much so.

The Location Script Breakdown

When the LM shows you a potential location, you need to know what's being proposed that you could shoot there. Kitchen scene? Garden? How many pages? Day? Night? Without this knowledge at your fingertips, how can you assess the potential of a given spot?

I carry this info with me in my notes. It's a simple location *script breakdown* which I will have by now either got from the ADs or have done myself. The breakdown lists how many pages I will be shooting in each location. I will have a summary page that ranks the locations *on a pages per basis*. In this manner I can tell at a glance where I'll be spending the most time shooting. Now I can prioritize the relative importance of a given location. There are numerous cases that defy this type of classification. "The Indians take the fort" is a classic example of a scene that will take far longer to shoot than its one-line description would otherwise rate. But there's nothing stopping me from placing this scene at the top of my priority list. It's my list.

So if we're scouting that mansion location, I have at my fingertips that we will be shooting:

Kitchen:	10 pages
Stables:	8 pages
Gardens:	4 pages
Entry:	1 page

This makes it easy to see what the priorities are. If I don't do this, someone on the location scout could fall in love with a great entry room where we're only shooting one page and I'll be under pressure to accept an otherwise poor location for that one minor point.

I will also have generated in my notebook a list of scenes — *by location* — with a short description of each. It reads like this:

Kitchen Scenes:

Scn 25. 3 pgs. Joe enters, prepares hot knish on countertop.

Scn 37. 4 pgs. Joe talks on phone to Emma, Sue enters, chases w/sword.

Scn 85. 2 pgs. Police question Sue at table, forensics photograph Joe.

This way, when we're on the location scout, while the other crew people are walking around making comments like *"Nice room,"* I can direct the group to assess the potential of the room in concrete script terms. *Joe dies here. Sue noshes there.*

Who Sits Where

On a location scout, the director sits in the front seat of the van beside the driver. It's partly a convention. A respect thing. It's also a visibility thing. You can see better in the front seat. Some directors make a big thing of it. I often find that I can get more done with the keys in the back seat. When I'm in the front I always end up with a stiff neck from turning around. Generally, on the early scouts, I'll take the front seat. We don't have that much to talk about yet. Later when it's just the LM, the DP, the designer and me, we can sit together and work.

Who Is Pitching You What?

When the van pulls up at a potential location, as director you're looking for a great backdrop for the actors and wonderful places that will bring your story to life. You assume that is everyone's top priority as well. But it often isn't.

The LM is looking for crew parking, unit parking, space for craft service, space for the caterers, the lunch tent, extras holding. They're also looking for potential neighbor problems, noise issues, shooting curfews. And, of course, expense.

The AD is looking for bogies. Is there an airport close by? Is the traffic hard to control? We lose shooting time waiting for sound. Do we have a long shuttle from the unit to set? We lose time shuttling the crew back and forth at lunch. Is the location sensitive? Does the crew have to wear booties to protect the floors? We lose time. Are the rooms small? Will the crew be bumping into each other?

The PM is looking for all of the above. Because all of this costs money. Money that won't appear on the screen. Money they won't have for your crane or your Steadicam. When the PM says, *"Hey, this is great…"* most times it will mean, *"Hey, this place works for the show."* But sometimes it will mean, *"Hey, this place works for the budget."*

Even the designer is not necessarily focused on your goals. They want a look that will fit into their vision for the show. They don't have to worry about moving actors through the set.

You, the director, have to build a solid wall between your right and left brains. You need to be able to build a door through that wall that you can slam and lock. When you are on the right side, there's only one question: Does shooting my movie here help or hinder the telling of this story? When you're on the left side, you're asking: What practical considerations could help or hinder my telling of the story in this place?

Once you get out of the van, you need to move fast. Opinions are being formed. First impressions sometimes crystallize into production decisions with dizzying speed. Location scouting is like shoe shopping. Some people take forever. Others are in and out of the store in a heartbeat. The only way to keep the high ground here is to be better prepared than anyone else and get in there first.

Walk Right In

I enter a given space knowing that the LM is showing it to me as the kitchen or dining room or whatever. But I remain open to considering the place as something else as well. The first thing I look for is the "thumbnail." The one angle that visually communicates what we're going to pretend this place is. If I'm making a scary thriller on a farm, I want to be able to put my viewfinder to my eye and see a really scary looking farm house. Or at least one that can be made to look so within our budget. There has to be a background for a great shot here. Otherwise why are we looking at it? The parking may be great. The parking is great at WalMart too.

Once I'm standing in front of that spot, I imagine the scene. I raise my viewfinder and rapidly visualize the action we'd be staging here. How does it work? Is there a beautiful shot? Is it too small, too big, too ugly?

I always shoot digital pictures of the potential locations. I try to frame and compose to reflect the actual shots I'll be shooting there. These photos are valuable at selling a location to a producer and for communication with the keys.

I often ask someone on the scout to stand in for me, a human body to help the framing. I point out the deficiencies from my point of view. If it's too small to shoot in, I say so right away. Ditto if it's un-cinematic. I try to avoid big arguments at this point, but if someone really starts pushing for an unworkable location, I'll usually play devil's advocate. I'll try and stage the scene right on the spot. Five times out of ten it becomes obvious to everyone why it won't work. The other five times I learn something.

And my eyes are always open to what else we can shoot there. What other scenes. Less moves = more movie.

It's a good general policy not to wax overly enthusiastic or pessimistic at this stage. If I know the LM has other choices, I ask to see them before I express a strong preference.

It's not my job to comment on the unit parking or the flights of stairs the gear needs to go up. I generally notice that stuff, but only use it if I need ammo to shoot down a bad location being pushed on me.

The Decision

The final decision as to where you shoot will be made based on a whole range of questions. It's a constant juggling act between aesthetics, cost and schedule.

Usually there's give and take. Sometimes the best location is just not affordable. That's where horse trading comes in. If it's between great and good, consider being flexible. But if it's between great and terrible, fight the fight. Don't over-compromise. After all, Mona Lisa framed against a background of a 15th century Italian stockyard just wouldn't be the same.

CASTING

Prep is now well under way. Many pots are simmering. Some on the back burner. Some beginning to boil. One issue you need to be on top of from early in prep is casting.

Non-insiders imagine casting to be one of the really great things about the director's job. Popular culture has it that the director casts his or her eye over the available field. He does a few lunches, perhaps considers making one young hopeful or another into a star. He accepts or rejects the plentiful casting couch invitations and finally nods this way or that. And it's suddenly all over *TMZ*. Back here on Earth, the majority of working directors often don't play much of a role in the star search.

So Where Do The Stars Come From?

On virtually all commercial films and TV shows, the stars are part of the financing package. The star cast is in place before the director is hired. That process frequently doesn't involve much or any involvement from the director. Are there exceptions? Sure. Do you personally know an approvable star on one of the lists who'll do the show? Great. Call the casting director. Put the name forward. Let them know you have a relationship. But supposing you don't know a listed star. You can still play, but it's a lot more difficult.

Every year there's a piece of brilliant casting that takes the audience by storm. Years back, when Mickey Rooney came out of virtual retirement to do *The Black Stallion*, scores of lapsed moviegoers came out and bought tickets to see an old friend. Madonna in *Desperately Seeking Susan*, Martin Sheen in *The West Wing*, Bill Murray in *Lost in Translation*, John Travolta in *Pulp Fiction*, Mickey Rourke in *The Wrestler*, Susan Sarandon in Lonely Island's *Mother's Night* — brilliant casting. None of these picks were obvious at the time. All of them were someone's great idea. There's no reason the next great idea can't be yours.

And Featuring….

Working directors generally have much more involvement in casting the non-starring roles. Most directors who have worked for any length of time have a group of favorite actors they like to cast regularly. The time to put those names forward is now, when you have your first phone conversation with the casting director. Be prepared. The casting director is in the midst of organizing a casting session for the actors auditioning for the smaller roles. Tell the casting director who you want to put up for consideration. They'll bring them in. Likewise, if there are actors you'd like to see read with other actors, now's the time to ask for it.

The casting director will very likely know the actors you're asking for and will usually be happy to bring them in. But if you snooze, you may very well lose. If the first casting session goes without your picks, you may never get another chance.

The Casting Session

Seasoned directors have cast many times. You may want to skim ahead. For the rest, here's an important note: Be on time. The schedule is often tight: 10 to 15 minutes per actor. You can create a real backlog by being only a few minutes late.

You will usually be sitting at a table. The assistant casting director will give you the session list and offer you liquid.

A camera will be set up to record the session for the executives who can't be there. And there's a monitor so you can watch how the actors photograph. Attending will usually be the director, the casting director, their assistant/s, someone to organize the arriving actors, and often one or more producers.

The first actor will be called in. They hand you their head shot and resume. They often want to shake hands. I don't much care either way, but some producers are concerned about germs and it can be sort of embarrassing. Most casting directors will establish a policy and try to stick to it, a *"Hi, we're not shaking"* sort of thing. If the actor hasn't read the entire script, a few comments from you regarding who/what/where their character is can be helpful. The assistant rolls camera. They have already slated, or the actor does, *"Hi, Jayne D'eau from Thespians-R-Us Talent, I'm reading for Blanche."* The assistant designated to read off-camera lines stands beside the camera to keep the eye line close. She reads the scene partner's dialogue. Away they go.

Watch the screen. Watch the actor. Listen. When they're finished, if they show some potential, ask for it again. Give them some simple direction: *"Try and internalize your pain, show me less but feel it more."* That sort of thing will show if they're flexible and directable.

This is one of my favorite parts of the whole business. It's like picking up a new instrument to see how it plays. When the actor has finished I try to find something positive and real to say about what they've offered up. I thank them and they leave. After they're gone I always ask for a minute to write down my reactions. I'll often compare them to a known actor. Things like, "*Matt Dillon-like. Not 100% but maybe.*" Otherwise, after we've auditioned twenty or thirty actors, they can start to blur.

Frequently when someone reads for one part, they'll seem better for another. Ask the casting director to have them wait outside. Confer, then the casting director can tell the actor what's going on and ask if they'd like to cold read or come back when we're doing call-backs. It's worth mentioning that frequently no one will be right for a particular role, but when you study your notes and the video later, you'll find the perfect choice in someone who read for a different role.

I try really hard to separate my personal response to the person from my calculated appraisal of their performance. All the audience ever sees is how the actor performs on the screen in this role. It matters not at all that they can chat cleverly to the director about whatever.

That being said, I also try really hard to be kind and have fun with them. I love actors. They put everything on the line. Of course they're disappointed if they don't get the job. So am I. But deep down we both know that casting is a quest for the perfect match between actor and role. And if someone is miscast, who's it going to help? Taken this way, casting can be a joy.

Call-Backs

It's rare to get everybody cast in one session. Perhaps the producers are elsewhere. Or some of the possible choices are on demos. You may need to see specific actors acting together. Or you're simply not sure. You do call-backs. Don't worry too much about inconveniencing the actors. The second best thing an actor can tell their friends is that they got a call-back.

When the session is over it's not unusual to discuss your reactions and picks. Frequently there's very little disagreement over most of the roles. It's often that obvious.

MEET THE STARS

When the star of the show is more important to the financing than the director, it can have a real impact on the star/director relationship. That's scary.

But look at it another way. *Top* stars have director approval. Top stars all want to work with the director *du jour*. In this case, they're working with *you*. This is a tremendous compliment.

Three Things Stars Want From Directors

1. Are you going to direct a film they will be proud of?

2. Can they trust you? Do you know what you're doing? Or is listening to you going to make them look really stupid?

3. Is the film you're making going to enhance or detract from their industry stature / commercial value?

Three Things Directors Want From Stars

1. Are they or can they become right for the part?

2. Are they prepared to trust me?

3. Are they here to do good work, or are they just paying the bills?

How Do You Find Out?

Although this discussion is aimed at directors, the ideas are equally useful to actors.

Screen their previous shows. Call other directors who have worked with this particular actor. As soon as they've officially been cast, ask the casting director to get their numbers from their agent. Call them up. Now that you've become familiar with their work, you won't have any trouble telling them how excited and honored you are to be working with them. This isn't too early to ask if they're concerned about anything. Give them your numbers. Tell them to call night or day. Set up a face-to-face meeting. Something really informal is often best, like a coffee or a drink.

Getting To Know You

I always find the first moment huge when I meet the person who is to be the star of my show. You know what they look like and act like on screen. But what are they "really like"?

The conversation will probably start with light stuff. You're both trying to get a sense of who the other is and why they're doing this. Both of you are in it for the art, the money, or some of each. How much of each is the question you're both here to find out.

It's great to get the conversation headed toward each of your respective points of view on the project. If the star feels the comedy you're directing is a dark tragedy, now would be a real good time to find that out.

In the first informal meeting it's worth asking your star what style of shooting they feel comfortable with. Long complex masters or cut-up coverage. Find out if they have a bad side to their face (many actors do) so you can plan the coverage accordingly. Likewise, it's good to know if they want their close-up first or last. It's worth telling them about your style and any unusual practices you might have. Lots of rehearsal, 2nd camera, etc.

By the same token, I try to give the star a very light version of some of my concerns. Like if the show is badly pressed for time. Or if there are ongoing script concerns that performance could help. Or if there's potential personnel problems (a difficult actor or producer).

I learned much of this from the wonderful and super talented Melissa Gilbert (*Little House on the Prairie*). Through our long working friendship, Melissa has given me insights into the dedicated actor's soul I otherwise would not have gained.

Melissa always advises me to be direct. So I attempt to give the star a quick way to read me. I'll tell them that I'm not a game player. I never have a secret agenda. I'm not a shouter (so don't wait for me to shout to know you're getting to me). And I won't ask for stuff I don't need. If on a rare occasion on set I say to the star, "*We're falling way behind, I need to do this one quickly and simply so we can spend time on the complicated stuff later,*" then I really mean it.

[With Melissa Gilbert filming ABC-TV's *Seduction*. Tina Schliessler photo]

The Many Others

Know what the actors say? *"How come directors don't care about me? They don't call, they often don't talk to me on set. What's with that?"* I call every single actor who's cast in a show of mine regardless of the size of their role. It's amazing how much "rainy night, overtime, freezing my ass off but have to perform" goodwill can be created with a simple, sincere "Welcome aboard, and thanks so much for joining our adventure!"

LOCATION PLANNING

By now we're well into prep. Casting is falling into place. The script is evolving nicely. Locations are being confirmed. Next step? I ask my AD to book me a series of mornings or afternoons or weekends to visit the confirmed locations alone. I take my script, palm top, cell phone, viewfinder, a comfortable chair, and if it's remote, something for lunch.

I enter a location, set up my chair, open the script, read the first scene and… wait.

I'm waiting to see the scene come to life before my eyes. Sometimes it takes an hour of re-reading, pacing the room, looking through the viewfinder from every angle. What am I looking for?

The Master

Most directors I know spend a good 80% of their time during location planning coming up with an interesting master shot for each scene. To me a master can be defined as follows:

The master shot is one continuous take that begins at the start of an entire or partial scene, ends at the end, and cinematically tells the entire story of the scene. Preferably without the need of any supporting coverage shots.

A good master has movement, rhythm, pace. It allows the cast to really act out and refine the scene before commencing the often confusing work of close-ups. By manipulating camera position and actor blocking, a good master alternates between wide view and close up. It is therefore very cut-able. It makes excellent use of the outstanding features of the location. And most importantly, it tells the story.

I read the scene. I then look for what's best in the location. What view tells the story of this location? What brought me here? When I help students out, it never ceases to amaze me how often emerging directors squander their location for no good reason. They'll read in the script that a four-some sits around a table after dinner drinking wine and talking. They'll walk into a location with a poor dining room but a fabulous living room. They'll create a shot looking into a corner with no room to move and nowhere to light from. When I mention that foursomes often drink wine sitting in a living room (not unlike this fabulous one right here, for ex-ample) I almost always get back, *"But the script says a dining room table."*

Or they'll start their shot looking at the interesting background but have their actors walk into a corner where they'll play the scene against a wall. I have been taught to find the best background and set the bulk of the scene *there*. Then plan backwards to find a good opening frame the ac-tors can pass through on the way to where it's great. Often it's as simple as moving a prop into position to create a good scene opening.

Let's say I'm doing location prep for a scene in a prison cell. I have a choice. I can shoot into the cell. In other words, I can set my scene to play against three walls and a toilet I could have built in the studio (so what am I doing out here on location?). Or I can wander into the back of the cell. I raise my viewfinder. I see that if I shoot this way my background is the central cell block. Layers and layers of cages. Cool.

So I've got my background. The direction the camera will be looking. Now I review the business of the scene. Let's say character X is painting a picture, Y enters, they talk, Y exits. I may look at the idea of starting the scene very close on the painting then track back as Y enters. I may plan for Y to come up behind X and remain behind him such that they are both more or less facing camera. I'll remain in that very interesting two-shot as they chat. Then I'll pan over and push in close on X for a scene end. I try it with my viewfinder. I look to see that there's room for the dolly. There's a simple, elegant master. I'll consider whether I want to try for close-ups as well if that fits the visual style. That's my scene.

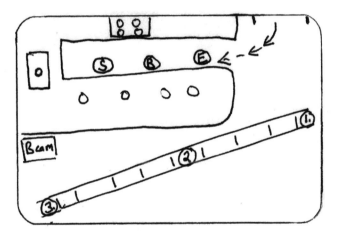

[Simple Plot Plan noting actor, track and camera positions.]

Next I'll sketch a simple *plot plan* of the location into my notebook. I copy that plan for as many scenes as I have on that particular set. Then for each scene I note dolly track location. I note 1st, 2nd, 3rd camera positions, actor positions, and so forth. In the database part of this file I'll note shot details, actor action, coverage plans, lens selections, etc. This is the key document that will provide most of the information I need to create my daily shot list.

On this plot plan I will also sketch in the precise location of all moveable decoration, furniture etc. I make certain the art department gets a copy so when I arrive on the shooting day the actors are walking where they should because I had set dec put the furniture where I wanted it to be. If I don't do this, I'll arrive on set on the day and the actors will block around the furniture the way set dec wants. In other words, the set decorator is directing my scene.

Now I photograph my location angles with the digital camera and make whatever notes I need to discuss with my keys. Planning this precisely reveals particular needs. I'll realize perhaps that we could use a neon sign for the dispensary over there: memo the art dept. I'll see we could use a lot more extras in the background: memo the AD. I'll see the walls are too close: memo camera dept for a wider angle. I'll see the armed guard stations in the corners: the actor should note them in his dialogue. Memo the writer. Memo the armorer.

I depart the location when I know pretty much what I'm going to do there. I've got enough info now to direct every department affected by my discoveries and my plans.

STORYBOARD?

Some directors storyboard everything. If it helps them visualize, great. In my experience the crew rarely looks at that stuff. Especially for the relatively inexperienced director, an elaborate director's package is a confusing waste of time — which is why so few do it. Their valuable prep time can be far better spent on things that will actually make a difference — like blocking a good master shot. In any case, storyboards of wide shots and close-ups of people talking are not all that expressive. One place storyboarding is very useful is in planning action scenes with a lot of coverage. Another is for effects-laden scenes.

There are two basic styles of storyboard: comic strip and shot list. Most storyboard artists favor the comic strip style. This is where the story flows from one panel to another cutting from wide shot to close-up to insert in the linear manner a comic book does. These boards are fun to read and they get their creator compliments. But unless there's a need to introduce and sell a new and complex sequence, and unless the director works closely with the artist, it's not just a waste of time. It gives an unacceptable degree of directorial control to a storyboard artist.

Here's a situation where the comic strip style worked well for me. I was doing an action picture with a scripted scene that had our heroine climbing from one apartment balcony to the next, evading a killer. The location we had was a beautiful old downtown hotel with a green copper roof — but no balconies. I was location planning alone up on the roof deck. I read and re-read the scene. I finally realized that the story beat was simply that we get the character to escape death in some cinematic way. I thought, *why not have her slide down the roof?* This was a 20-story building.

I made some notes. I drew some boards. I went to the producer. His response to my verbal pitch: "*No way, far too expensive. How we gonna do that?*" I showed him my storyboards. Five minutes later he was booking the stunt doubles and ordering up the special rigs.

[Storyboard roof sequence from Republic Pictures' *Breach of Trust.*]

[Storyboard roof sequence from Republic Pictures' *Breach of Trust.*]

[Storyboard roof sequence from Republic Pictures' *Breach of Trust*.]

It was a remarkable sequence. I'm proud of it. Check it out at *http:// charleswilkinson.com/resume.php?type=feature* under the *Breach of Trust* tab.

The second type, the "shot list" style of storyboard, is used to explain the director's intentions for an already scripted, complex action sequence where there's to be a significant contribution from Stunts, FX, Visual FX, and/or maybe 2nd Unit. It's important to spell out your intentions to the team.

These boards are what the name implies. They are an illustrated shot list. What I do is draw a stick man frame of the first master shot. If it's a moving shot, I'll show 1st frame, middle, and end. Then I'll draw and list the coverage, the close-ups, inserts, and so forth for that segment of the scene. Then the next master. Then the subsequent coverage. I do them in what I anticipate will be shooting order.

When the boards are done I'll schedule a meeting with Stunts, FX, and/ or Visual FX, present them with my plan and ask them for input. I notice the team tends to get way more creative when there's a coherent plan to work from, rather than when we're starting from scratch in a group think. Once the action team has reached a consensus, I incorporate changes and issue revised boards. I copy all the affected departments and note the areas that will be affected; props, wardrobe, transport, locations, etc.

An Imperfect Plan

It goes without saying that you'll miss wonderful stuff in prep. You always arrive on set with a less than perfect plan. But in the high pressure of production, there's only one thing worse than an imperfect plan — no plan at all.

The location planning I do becomes the shot list I take to set on the day. I present it to the DP as a starting point. The DP will almost always have ideas to enhance mine or completely replace them with something better. Great. Often an actor will suggest a blocking change that's vastly superior. Terrific. While it's fun to inspire in the crew a sense of confidence, I'm not there to be right. I'm the first one to abandon my carefully made plan if something better comes along. But I watch the blocking process carefully. If I sense it's spinning out of control, if we're starting to fall behind, I have a back-up plan — the shot list based on my prep notes.

Saving Time For What?

If I'm making all these production decisions in prep on my own without the expert creative input of my keys, what am I doing on set? Isn't that supposed to be the creative crucible of filmmaking? Depends on your POV. Some directors think directing is about where to put the camera. I personally think that's a very small part of the job. Of course a director needs to acquire technical fluency, and yes, location planning is mostly about technical considerations. But I believe that *prep* is where the director puts their stamp on the look of the show. If the director preps properly, by the time the shooting schedule commences, the DP can take it from there on set.

Which leaves the director free to do what he/she is there for. To work with the actors. To watch that each of the critical story beats is coming across. To feel the mood of the scene. To sense the pacing, the tone. In short, to tell the story. If you prep right, you will carve out for yourself the calm detachment that on-set creativity depends on.

The Night Before

Prep ends. Usually much too soon. But ready or not, the evening will come when you set your alarm clock and turn in for one last good sleep before the madness of production commences. Tomorrow is the first day of shooting.

Sweet dreams.

[With Frank Irvine, Dionne Luther, and Robert Clothier on *The Beachcombers*. Tina Schliessler photo]

chapter nine

SHOOTING

"We shot a feature all morning, a TV movie all afternoon, and Reality TV for the last hour of O.T." — Common film set complaint.

A typical working director's day begins hours before call. If set (shooting) call is at 7 a.m., and crew call is at 6 a.m., count backwards. One hour of driving to set, 45 minutes shot list writing, 30 minutes for exercise, shower, dress, and breakfast. Alarm clock set at 4:45 a.m. Really.

My routine during production is I wake up, do the personal prep, boot the computer and launch into my shot list. Here is what my shot list looks like, actual size.

DAY SEVEN DECOUPAGE

1.   SCENE 13 - WAREHOUSE CHASE

Up at Real Door

Action: REAL Mac comes through real door, wavers, lunges onto genie lift

Camera: On the ground, low angle **- B cam C/U, C Cam up behind Mac.**

2.   M/S reveal Morgan up on real door - B cam C/U, C Cam up behind Morgan

3.   Stunt 'Mac' real jump to post - 2 cams down, one up

4.   Stunt 'Morgan' swings off - 2 camsdown, one up

5.   Insert post bends

6.   Mac c/u lands, runs to stairs

7.   Mac on stairs M/S pan, & B cam XCU feet, face.

[Typical shot list.]

How do I come up with this info?

The call sheet says first up is Scene 13. Read Scene 13 in your script. Make notes of the key story beats. If it's important that Morgan is trying to sneak up on Mac, that's a story beat. If he fingers the gun in his pocket, that's a beat. If he's secretly scared — a beat. Then open your location file. Review your plot plan and shooting plan. Then start writing the shot list for that scene.

Who are you writing this info for? Who gets a copy? You, the DP, the AD, the key grip, the gaffer, the sound department, the script supervisor, possibly the PM. Call sheet aside, your shot list is the real menu for the day.

Shot lists vary from director to director. My personal shot list first notes what scene we are cutting from so I'll know what the tone is. It notes what the cut in and the cut out is. I'll list the master shot, whether it's on track, sticks, Steadicam. I'll note if the shot goes from scene beginning to end. I'll note the story beats this shot must express.

I will note what B camera is doing. Often B cam notes will be less specific, leaving B more open to creative improv.

Then I'll list any coverage I may desire, the close-ups and inserts. I note what part of the scene they will cover and what story beat must be expressed.

That's it. End of scene. Move on to what's next on the call sheet.

I number each set-up. When I get to the end of the call sheet, if I find I have 25 setups and if I know from the previous day's work (or if this is day one from soliciting the opinions of my keys on what they think the unit is capable of) that our unit can only do 20 set-ups without overtime, I know I either have to scale back or plan for overtime.

It's common for a director to put what's known as a "target of opportunity" on their shot list. On the off chance you finish early or can't film something you'd hoped to, the AD will be prepared to shoot your target.

For the crew version of my list I'll strip off all the cut from, cut to, story beat info and make up a simple shot list for the crew. I'll print a copy of each, cut it to fit in my pocket, and I'm out the door.

THE CIRCUS

The unit. That assembly of production trucks, trailers, catering vans, extras holding tents, generators, picture cars, crew cars, and equipment carts. This is what is known as "The Circus." With good reason. Before people went to the movies (or watched TV) they went to the circus. The circus brought the sights, sounds, and smells of exotic foreign worlds into the lives of people who frequently never traveled more than a few miles from home their entire lives. Circus folk were exotic. They dressed outlandishly, behaved outrageously, and often had morals that could make a rabbit breeder blush. In other words, your average film set.

There will be a map on the back of the call sheet directing you to where the circus is today. As you draw near you'll see signs directing you to crew park and to the set.

You've Arrived

I first seek out the 3rd AD and give her a copy of the crew shot list for copying and distribution. She usually gives me pocket-sized sides (the scenes we're shooting this day). If catering is up I'll get a coffee, compliment the caterers on yesterday's lunch, and ask what's on for today. Caterers love food. When you take an interest they will cook for you. Next I'll meet and greet whoever is around and then head up to set.

The First Look

It's never right. There is always something happening on your set when you first see it in the morning that, left unchecked, will cost you time and set-ups later in the day.

No matter how thoroughly you've briefed the crew on where the scene is or where the camera is going to be or where is safe to stow gear or how the furniture is arranged, invariably something is not where it should be. Get there early and it's no problem. A simple word to the FX guys that their smoke tube will be in shot and presto, it's gone and you've made a friend.

I walk through my sets visualizing each of the scenes looking through my viewfinder. This is my first time seeing it dressed. It looks different. Maybe my plan was flawed. Maybe the other side of the room is better in this light. I'll often ask the set dressers to flip the furniture in a set. Again if I'm there early, no problem.

If there are critical props on the set I will usually oversee their placement personally. The location of the pots and pans impacts on where the cutting board will be. Which impacts on where the murder weapon would likely be. If I don't make certain it's all where it should be, we'll get to staging that part of the scene later in the day and the actor will say, "*But why would the knife be there?*" And there goes the time I need for one of my precious set-ups.

Welcoming The Cast

I always ask my AD department to alert me when various people arrive. I like to meet the DP and designer to talk about yesterday's dailies and to go over the work in front of us today. But most important, I need to know when the actors arrive at the circus.

I make it a point to seek out all the actors just to say hi each morning. But I actually visit with the lead actors when they arrive. Even if we're already shooting a scene they're not in. I'll make the effort to slip away during a lighting break. Why? Because it's a mark of respect. Plus I like most actors enormously. Plus... *they are what the audience sees! They are telling my story!* Camera angles and great music mean little without a high-performance actor. If I have to, I'll settle for average in any department but acting. If the actor is uncomfortable, if they don't believe the words, if they're angry at their costumer — it *shows!* Five minutes chatting with the leads as they're in makeup, asking how their kids are at home, talking about a particularly good performance in last night's dailies, sharing a worry about today's line-up. This is not a huge sacrifice to make for the magic they bring us each day.

During the few moments I spend greeting the leads each morning I may also use the opportunity to bring them up to speed on my approach to what's up first. If it's a straightforward scene in a location we both know I may ask the actor to give me their blessing to go ahead and block it without them. So they can remain in hair/make-up/wardrobe and thus get to camera faster. We've just saved 30 minutes. I'm one or two set-ups ahead.

TIME TO ROLL

I'll often walk or ride up to set with the 1st AD. It gives us a chance to go over the first few scenes.

When we arrive on set, all the pre-rigging should be done. Usually the DP will be there a few minutes before set call. Together the DP and I will visit the set alone. We'll quickly discuss our approach to the scene. This isn't just a start of day thing. I need this time alone with the DP prior to every scene.

The 1st AD will then say something like: *"Ding, ding. We're on the clock. Welcome to day (# whatever) of the fabulous production of (whatever). Our first deal, scene 11. In the study. John and Sue argue, Sue goes boo hoo. Charles, it's all yours."*

Show time.

This is it. What I do next will have an unchangeable impact on what the audience sees.

I generally say something like, *"Morning, all. At this point in the story, Sue and John are quarrelling. Sue has just heard John making a date with Ellen. Now in this scene we have John seated by the phone, having just hung up. Sue enters, paces, arguing. The set works best for light and background if we seat John somewhere around here and if we have Sue enter here and pace in this general area facing this way. The camera will be on this side, moving in slowly. Any comments? OK, let's have a look. Blocking, and action."*

The actors will try a run-though and I'll watch it looking through my viewfinder. I move as I intend the camera to move. The keys will watch us, each with a view to what impact my plan will have on their department. When the actors experience difficulty with some aspect of the set, we'll pause and resolve the issue then move on.

Once we're through it I'll mention my coverage plans, close-ups here, inserts there. The DP will often have suggestions. Perhaps the cast will volunteer something. We'll adjust and then run it again. The 1st AD will advise the camera assistant that, *"This time it's for marks."* We will stop and start the action, giving the assistant a chance to put a mark down where we wish an actor to pass through or stop. Each actor gets their own color of mark.

Once we finish this, the 1st AD will ask the DP if he's seen enough to rig it. If so, the AD sends the cast away and says, "*The crew has the floor.*" The DP commences (or finishes if it's been pre-rigged) lighting the shot.

Once the cast finishes with hair/make-up/wardrobe, if the set is not yet ready, this is the time we'll get together and rehearse. We'll go to the green room, or our chairs, or out in a field, and run it and run it. If there are problems we'll try to work them out (more on that later). If not we'll run it until it's working. By which time the AD will be calling us back to set.

Ready, Aim….

The actors take their places. The AD calls for final touches. Hair, make-up and wardrobe slip in and check the details. The director takes a seat at video village in front of the video monitors that display the working cameras. The sound boom person gets into position. The camera operator and focus puller mount up onto the dolly. The dolly grip pushes the dolly to first position. The DP takes a final light reading and calls out the exposure to his 1st assistant. The AD will call, "*Roll sound.*" The mixer will confirm he's recording, the boom man will announce, "*Speed.*" The AD will call, "*Roll camera.*" The first assistant will start the camera and respond, "*Camera rolling, mark.*" The 2nd or 3rd camera assistant will hold up the correctly marked slate, call out the scene and take numbers and say "*Mark.*" They'll smack the clapper (although this is starting to become less common). The operator/s will set the opening frame, then call out "*Frame.*"

Now it's your turn. "*And… action.*" The "and" is not an affectation. You're giving the cast and crew a few milliseconds to ramp up to speed rather than simply barking "action" and expecting everything to begin at once.

DIRECTING AS THE CAMERAS ROLL

The scene commences. The director watches the monitors. What exactly is the director watching for? There are so many people watching. The DP is watching for light, focus, and operation. The sound people are listening for clarity and overlaps. The script supervisor is watching to see that all the lines are delivered and who picks up what prop when. What's left for the director to watch for?

What I'm looking for is, do I like this movie? Do I get what's going on? Does this shot fit into the movie? Am I learning something important I did not know before this moment? Are the story beats clear enough? Do I understand what the actors are saying? Do I understand what they really mean?

The director is the only one on set who is actually watching the movie like the audience will.

The director is the proxy audience. The director is the audience's lawyer. If I as the director don't feel that something on screen serves my client's (the audience's) best interests — I object.

In the first take or two of the master, especially if it's a long scene, I will count the things that need improvement. That makes it easier to remember when I'm talking to the cast and crew between takes.

Who Gets To Say "Cut"?

The director. No one else. Unless there's imminent danger to life and limb, no exceptions.

When the take is over or something goes seriously wrong, the director calls out *"cut"* and filming stops. Sometimes in a long take an actor will blow a line. Sometimes I'll call out *"keep rolling,"* and have the script supervisor prompt them. If the shot is what we call a "one-er," that is the entire scene shot in one uncut take with no close-ups or insert shots, when there's a mistake I cut and go again. But if I'm shooting coverage it's a judgment call. Some actors don't like being directed while the camera is rolling. Ask first.

That Was Perfect — We're Going Again

Once you call cut you're faced with the decision of whether to take it again or move on. Your decision is based on whether you thought the actor's performances told the story believably and got the point across. It's also based on how well the take worked from the key's various POVs.

Of course you were keeping a third eye out for everyone else's stuff during the take.

When an operator or a sound person tells me the take was no good, that means they want another. It's a good idea to ask, "*which part was no good?*" Say this was a long master for which we'll be shooting coverage. If the flaw was at a point where I think we'll be into close-ups and if we're in a hurry, we move on. This can be a contentious area. We'll talk more about it later.

I'll often have notes for the camera operator. Delay this move. Pan over to catch her entrance faster, that sort of thing. I'll sometimes have blocking notes for the actors. More often I'll have insights into what they're trying to express and how to better express it. I give the notes and we go again.

How Demanding Can You Be?

Nothing is ever perfect. The cast always wants to do another. So does the camera operator. So does sound. But they generally have a less acute awareness of the pressures of time. On the other hand, if you habitually finish the day ahead of schedule, the keys and the actors are going to be rightly concerned that you're not getting their best.

Working With The Director of Photography

Many directors consider their on-set relationship with the DP to be the key creative relationship in the entire show. A friendly professional interaction is critical to both the smooth functioning of the set and to the look and feel of the finished film. The most complex emotions and the most subtle story beats are invisible without brilliant lighting, camera movement, framing, and exposure. But as with any intense relationship there is great potential for both harmony and conflict between the director and the DP.

I learned an important lesson on my first film. The DP and I fought like cats and dogs. He felt I didn't care about the look of the show. I felt he was working too slowly, essentially shooting his demo reel. We were both wrong. What we had neglected to do was sit down and agree upon how much time we had for each scene and stick to a schedule based on that. I was nervous. I think I probably pushed too hard, even when we were ahead.

Since then I've learned how to establish a *modus vivendi* with DPs. We essentially negotiate the ratio we're going to set between work time and shoot time. So I never have that situation you see on student sets so often where 95% of the time goes into building and lighting the shot, then the director is rushed to do one or two quick takes and move on.

Every director/DP combo finds its own way to rock. Some DPs feel it's their job to design all the shots and some directors are happy to let them. Some directors design every shot and the DP lights. Whatever works. The important thing is communication and for there to be a clear understanding that *shotmaking is secondary to storytelling.* The look of the show is super important, but how often do you hear a movie patron or critic saying, "*Hey, the story sucked and the acting blew, but man — what camera moves! Two thumbs up!*"

Finally, it's worth mentioning that there's an attitude some DPs have that doesn't fit real well into the collaborative enterprise that filmmaking is. Fortunately that rarely happens. Most director/DP relationships are strong, creative partnerships that span years.

[With DP Tobias Schliessler on *Quarantine.*
Chris H. Benz photo]

Working With Stunts And FX

Stunts and FX people love their work. They're often like big kids in a sand-box. The enthusiasm most of them bring to your show can be infectious. But sometimes they're so anxious to give you their best that they're inclined to give too much. It's a rare stunt man or FX worker who offers up <u>less</u> than you want. Left to their own devices they generally go for bigger, louder, harder, faster. A popular FX crew shirt says, "*F!#$ the dialogue — Let's blow something up!*" Unless you let them know your intent in the action scenes, don't be surprised if they propose putting a car chase gun battle into *The King's Speech.* If the script says: "*Jim has a heart attack*," don't let them give you three back flips with full-on chest exploding blood hits.

Working With Visual FX

This is far too complex a topic to even brush over here. And it changes from day to day as new technology comes on line. Many shows have vi-sual FX. Some shows are so full of computer generated imagery (CGI) that the actors are shot against a screen and everything else is done in post. There will be one or more Visual FX consultants on-set when the FX-oriented scenes are being filmed. Because the shooting for comput-erized processing is so precise, the director can find themselves a by-stander on their own set.

The way to approach this is to understand that the Visual FX crews work for the FX lab. It's in the FX lab's interest that you, the director, under-stand their process. They're usually happy to give you the tour, the demo, even a full-on workshop. They welcome you to come sit in the corner and watch. Learn the rules. Direct the story. Because a weak performance surrounded by 30,000 awesome robots is still a weak performance.

That's Lunch

Lunch always comes too soon. There are union rules covering lunch is-sues. Say you're in the middle of a shot when lunchtime comes and you haven't got a useable take yet. The AD asks the crew shop steward for something called "Grace." If granted, this allows the director to try and get a useable take in a few more tries.

Once the unit breaks they take either a half hour or a full hour counted from the time the last person through the line is served. Lunch length is a crew-negotiated issue. From a director's point of view, hour-long lunches are bad. All the energy drains out of the crew. We eat too much, start to snooze, then take an hour to get back up to speed.

The first people through the lunch line at the catering truck are usually the teamsters. They always park their clubhouse on wheels strategically between craft service and catering.

The next people to appear in the lunch line are the day actors. Most of the cast is mind-numbingly idle most of the time. When it's lunch, they're there like… like actors at a catering truck.

Next, the crew that happened to find themselves close to the catering truck when lunch was called surge in. Next, the set cast and crew. The director is in there somewhere.

Resist the urge to crash the line. The people in the food line will often offer you the chance to move ahead of them. Don't do it. As polite and friendly as their gesture may be, there's a risk you'll be seen as thinking you're more important than they are. If you really need to do stuff at lunch, ask your AD to have a plate made up and sent to your trailer ahead of time.

At lunch I always check messages, call home and do any producer calls I need to do. My family likes to hear from me. And producers often like to hear how stuff is going from the horse's mouth.

[At lunch with Denise Crosby on *Max*. Kharen Hill photo]

We're Back

The director and AD will have spoken during the break. We will have discussed how far ahead or behind we might be for the day. If we feel we're behind, it's often good to get the first shot of the afternoon done quickly. It lets the food know we mean business about digestion. And it sets a pace for the afternoon.

That first morning went by in a bit of a blur. We didn't have much time to talk about shooting style. Let's do that now.

THE DIRECTOR'S MEDIUM

Obviously, every director has a different artistic style. And each script calls for a different stylistic approach. Stylistic issues are generally thought to be a function of the artistic needs of the story, and especially the talent of the director. That's why Ridley Scott gets paid more than the director who did *Gladys the Talking Mule*, right?

The reality that working directors know to be so true is that business pressures frequently play a greater role in the artistic realization of a project than… well, art.

Those who have never been in the trenches as a hired director rarely have much awareness of this. What film or TV critic ever blames budget or schedule or network issues for a show's shortcomings? How often does a reviewer invest the two minutes it would take on IMDb.com to learn that all of this producer's other shows have been critical failures and that this current director actually managed to rise above.

Shooting Style

A director who has 15 days to shoot a 90-minute TV movie must adjust the pace of work to fit that schedule. But the director must also consciously adopt a shooting *style* to fit that schedule. The most common shooting style for a project like this would be a simple "master/coverage" style. A master shot with close-ups.

A director who has 80 days to shoot a studio film has the luxury to choose a different style, a common one being what is sometimes referred to as the "sub-master" style. This is where an overall master may not be shot at all. Instead a series of sub-masters are shot for each emotionally different section of the scene. Then appropriate coverage (two-shots, close-ups, inserts, etc.) is shot for each sub-mastered section. Obviously this technique is much more time-consuming. It's also much more capable of finding the subtle emotional beats as the characters act and react throughout the scene.

Shooting style also changes with different cast and crew members. A difficult actor, or one with a poor memory for lines or marks, is not going to give their best in a long, complex master. Likewise, a camera department with a less than gifted operator or focus puller is not going to give their best with those aesthetically beautiful long lenses one might otherwise use.

A relatively new style of shooting has developed as the younger, video-trained directors start working. Not having grown up respecting the cost of film, and frequently advancing so fast as to not learn how intelligent blocking advances the story, some directors simply "hose it down" from all angles and hope for the best. Particularly in many of the newest action flicks the directors are telling their DPs to light, so shooting from all angles is possible. Then they go in with many cameras and open fire. Crossing the axis is not a concern to this type of director. It will be interesting to see if this style endures. When one re-visits the effortless-seeming but extraordinarily graceful blocking Mike Nichols employs in *The Graduate* or *Who's Afraid of Virginia Woolf?*, one can't help but wonder if there's a relationship between the jerky, axis-crossed impulse cutting of modern blockbusters and the increasingly common response young people give when you ask if they've seen *Transformers*: "*Oh yeah... I've seen part of it....*"

What Cast and Crew Wants

Many actors and directors prefer long, complex master shots that make use of only a limited amount of coverage. A long master gives them a chance to create a mood, control the pace, tell the story. By contrast, cutting a scene up into short takes makes it more difficult to maintain emotional continuity and progression. Crews respect intelligent master shots. Because they require skill and training to execute.

Ideally one would shoot a cinematic master, then shoot just enough coverage to allow the scene to be adjusted for pace, meaning and emphasis later on in post. Why doesn't everybody shoot this way?

Obviously, no director intentionally sets out to shoot a boring master. But trying to do otherwise is really challenging. What if you invest a morning in blocking, lighting, and rehearsing a complex master only to find that an actor keeps blowing a line or missing a mark? What if your operator just can't make the camera move. Or your focus puller keeps getting it soft? What if you get up to Take 15, they can't get it right but insist on doing it over and over until they do? Over and over and over. …

Some directors respond to this fear by risking little with their master. They'll put most of their effort into cutting it up into bite-sized pieces. They concentrate on getting enough coverage to make it happen in editing. One of my favorite executive producers, Don S. Williams, used to refer to this shooting style as the "*monkey at the typewriter*" approach.

A more cinematic method is to commit to as intelligent a master shot as seems realistically achievable within the constraints of the project, and then cover as needed.

Master/Coverage

When you're channel-surfing on your TV, master/coverage is recognizable at a glance. Every scene starts close on a phone or something, then pulls back into a static wide shot. Cut to medium close-up. Ping pong back and forth on medium close-ups for a while. Then into close-ups. Back out to the static master once to remind us of the geography. Then cut to close on the actor's pensive stare for scene end.

The argument is made that it's the safest way of filming actors saying and doing stuff such that a general audience will get the general drift. But much more than that: it is an industrial system. In the same way that an automobile assembly line is. When producers demand coverage, they are demanding components. Engines, fuel pumps, tail lights.

In this system the real act of "creation" happens mainly in the editing room, when the various components are assembled. The components can be assembled in many different ways. Some of them far from anything the director ever imagined.

Creative Coverage

There are tricks to make coverage more interesting. One is to block the scene with a lot of business. Instead of two people sitting talking, have one or both of them busy clearing off the dishes from the table or reading the paper, knitting, watching TV, pacing. Anything appropriate to the mood. If the subject is moving, the close-ups are automatically more dynamic. And if the actors have business, you can always cut away to an insert of the knitting or whatever, which will often redefine what's really going on in the scene.

A second camera can work wonders with coverage. If you have two cameras and if you must shoot master/coverage, it's often not possible to shoot a good close-up angle on an actor with the B cam while the A cam is shooting the master. The B can rarely get a perfect angle. The light is usually wrong. Frequently the A cam drifts into B's frame on the dolly. So what does the B cam do while A shoots the master? It goes fishing.

The director can ask the B cam operator to try interesting moves. The kinds of creative shots you'll never have time to set up and execute properly with the A cam. In this way you just may get some very spontaneous and creative shots. You may also get a lot of re-frames, out-of-focus shots, and unusable material. But the trade-off is often well worth it.

One major caution with this strategy. Be straight with your sound people. If your hope is to get the scene in an interesting master with some exciting B camera grabs, quietly let the sound mixer know that. Otherwise they'll assume you are shooting close-ups and may not be as fussy over sound quality on the master. More than once I've felt joy telling the unit we've just shot a terrific one-shot scene and then looked up to see a freaked-out sound mixer storming over sputtering, *"But... you said...."*

Pulling The Plug

Airplane pilots have a decision point picked out on the runway before they commence take-off. They know that if they're not airborne by that point, they have just enough runway left for a panic stop. Continuing to attempt take-off beyond the decision point *might* result in a successful take-off. It could also result in a fiery death.

A director facing the complex master situation needs a decision point as well. To decide how much time to invest in blocking, lighting, and shooting a complex master, the director needs to discuss with the AD what the maximum time shooting this scene can take. Let's say you've got to be out of it by 4 p.m. Calculate how much time you'd need to abandon the plan and shoot enough coverage to get the scene. Say that's three hours. So 1 p.m. is your decision point.

As you near 1 p.m., questions need to be asked and answered. How close are they to getting it? Say it's Take 6 and you've already got a couple of otherwise useable takes with some minor problems. If both cast and crew are performing well, you're in pretty good shape. Quietly tell your AD if we don't get it in two or three more takes, we'll move on.

[Prepping for action. Tina Schliessler photo]

The Let Down

It's hard to pull the plug on a sequence like this. The cast and crew have a tendency to interpret your pragmatic choice as a vote of non-confidence in them. They feel they've failed the director. Occasionally operators will plead or actors will demand another one. For the young director faced with an experienced cast or crew, this situation can be intimidating.

But the director is the pilot. Pilots don't poll their passengers to see who needs to get there so badly they're prepared to take unacceptable risks.

Working With Sound

Which brings us to another common director/crew conflict: sound. The sound mixer sits at a little cart off to one side. Sometimes in another room entirely. They watch the camera feed on a monitor. But their real window on the world is their headphones. They communicate with their boom operator via a small talk-back mic. Sound mixers often act like they're not part of the unit. There's a good reason. They have to be "blind" and apart.

Humans are visually oriented. We pay far more attention to the sensory input we receive through our eyes than that which we receive through our ears. Most people on and off a film set know very little about sound. Few people listen very closely to sound in real life. But put them in front of a movie and watch how quickly they get restless if the sound is muggy. Or if the dialogue is hard to understand, distorted, out of sync.

On set it's rare that anyone will complain if the DP says we need 30 minutes to put up more lights. But let the sound mixer ask for five minutes to put up a blanket or adjust a radio mic and suddenly we're under the gun. We gotta roll. Come *on*.

There's always pressure to relegate sound issues to the back burner. This can be a terrible mistake. There is no substitute for good location sound. Crew people often say, "*You can't ADR the picture. Dub it later.*" And on a giant-budget show this is almost true. But for the majority of shows, if you get poor dialogue recorded on set, the show will suffer badly. The reason is simple. Looping, ADR (automated dialogue replacement), is difficult and expensive to do well. People may tell you different. They're mostly wrong. Here's why.

Looping

Looping (so called because the actual film used to be spliced into a loop so it could run through the projector over and over again) goes like this: it's 9 a.m. An actress comes into the studio with a cup of coffee. She's greeted by the engineer and the sound editor. Frequently the director is off directing their next show. The engineer hands the actress a list of lines that need replacing. The actress enters the booth and stands up to the mic. She's asked for a few words to get a sound level. Then the engineer hits play. The actress watches herself on the screen. She listens to the original line that needs replacing. She watches it once or twice, then says she's ready. The engineer hits record. The actress watches the screen and attempts to say the line with the exact same pacing and spacing as she did when it was filmed. She'll take it a number of times. Occasionally the editor might say something like, *"Try one with a bit more feeling."* Once they get one that seems to fit *visually* it's on to the next loop. What's wrong with this picture?

Looping Turns Everything Into a Foreign Film

Cinephiles often refuse to watch foreign films that have been dubbed into English. The reasons are obvious. The original performance is lost forever, replaced by someone with a cup of coffee standing in a booth at 9 a.m. Exterior scenes are recorded *inside* and they sound that way. Scenes shot in a giant hall are recorded in a tiny booth and they sound that way. A scene that was shot with a number of actors guided by a director, feeling the set, feeling each other, feeling the pure chemistry of a group performance, screaming, whispering, laughing — all this is gone forever.

On high-budget shows the studio can demand that the performances be re-created. The mixing facility will have the money to pull in all kinds of hi-tech resources. So much talent and money is thrown at the problem that they can get really close to what was lost. And the actors get the time and direction to recreate their performance, sometimes even to improve it. But many less-expensive shows are running low on budget by the time they get to post sound. The effort is almost never made.

We often shoot in locations that for one reason or another have not been chosen with good clean sound in mind. We often haven't got time to re-take indefinitely until there's a clean sound take. But anyone who's spent much time on set knows that there's a tendency to denigrate the importance of location sound. People who have never spent five minutes in a looping session will say, "*It's good enough for guide track. Gotta move on.*"

What a good director does is establish a dialogue with the sound mixer. Make it a habit to include the sound guys in your blocking discussions. Suggest mic placement if it's a difficult angle and the mixer is receptive. Tell the mixer when you shoot a wide master and tight B cam coverage on the same take, a mixer's nightmare because he can't get the boom in close. Chose to either radio mic the B cam subject or do another one on B cam alone. And finally, in a case where you don't have time to do it right for sound, explain why and hope for their best under difficult circumstances.

THE SCRIPT SUPERVISOR

The script supervisor or continuity person is responsible for continuity. Which hand held the drink? What should the clock say? That sort of thing. Keeping track of all these details in a moving scene with a half dozen actors can be very demanding for her (the overwhelming majority of script supervisors are women, no idea why). But that's not all the script supervisor is doing.

They are also following each line of dialogue in the script. If an actor misses or changes a line, the script supervisor notifies the director. Frequently the director will empower the script supervisor to prompt the actors during a take when they forget their lines.

On top of this, they are responsible for making extensive notes in the script and in the logs they turn in to the editor. Those notes include how many takes of each shot were done, what parts of the scene were covered by what shots, what lens and aperture were used, what camera roll, sound roll, and any relevant production notes. In editing, all of the information the editor has about everything on the shoot comes through the script supervisor. Tough job.

Be friends with your script supervisor.

Because they make the notes, they are the messenger. So the script supervisor is sometimes blamed for the message by producers and network executives. "*Why the hell didn't you shoot a close-up? How the hell did that line get changed?*" A script supervisor can react to these unreasonable pressures by passing them on to the director. In TV it's not uncommon for the script supervisor to adopt the role of script cop. They can pop up and ask for another take whenever something happens they know they'll get hell for. This can seriously impact on a director's spontaneity.

A common battleground is the *overlap* issue. When two or more people are talking, it's natural for them to interrupt each other. To overlap their words on top of each other's. Script supervisors (and sound mixers) are trained to hate overlaps. Because it makes sound editing more difficult. If you're shooting a close-up of Mary and we hear Andy's dialogue on top of hers, how does the editor cut for performance and pacing? But when the director intends to run the shot uncut, overlaps are often OK. It's extremely irritating to have the script supervisor constantly requesting additional takes because of overlaps. I ask the actors to "watch the overlaps" when we're shooting coverage. But when we're doing one-shot sequences, I advise the script supervisor to check with me before speaking up. And simply make the note on her report that the director was advised of this particular continuity crime and chose to accept it. This at least solves the problem for the short term.

A far better solution is to get the script supervisor on your team. Think about it. They sit right beside the director at the monitor all day. They have a better vantage point from which to watch and understand the director's approach than anyone else on set. If the director were to choose one best friend on set, who better?

I always have a meeting with the script supervisor in prep, even on an episodic TV show. I let them know I value and respect their opinion. I tell them I see our working relationship as a collaboration. I invite them to have fun with me on the show. More often than not this results in me having someone to bounce stuff off on set. Someone without a vested interest I can ask for advice on a particular take. And if I get into trouble

I have a second brain helping me dig out. In short, the script supervisor is both *at* my side and *on* my side.

COOL TOOLS — DIRECTOR PROTOCOL

Who hasn't seen images of James Cameron riding in the submarine down to the Titanic? Most photos of directors have them standing with gear, eye to the Panaflex, riding the dolly.

You as the director have the authority to look through the camera and re-frame, re-compose, anytime you want. You have the authority to ride the dolly, the crane, the chopper, sometimes even the stunt car. But there's a fairly rigid protocol.

The Rules for The Tools

1. Don't hurt anyone.

2. Don't waste time.

3. Don't make a fool of yourself.

That's it. All the observations that follow are illustrations of how to follow these rules. Seasoned directors may want to skim most of this.

Looking Through The Camera

Should you look through the camera? After all, video village is comfortable. You can see what the operator has framed in your monitor. Why interfere with the camera crew? The obvious answer is that sometimes it's faster and easier to *show* the operator than to tell them.

The protocol is as follows: as a shot is being set up, wait for the grips and the camera assistants to set the camera up where it's going to be. On the tripod, on the dolly, wherever. Stand near the camera to let them know you want a look. But give them time and space to set up and level it. This is where the operator will ask you what lens you'd like to see. Once the operator begins looking through the camera, but before they get the assistant to start getting focus marks, ask them, "*Can I have a quick look, please?*"

[Deano and Tobias in "The Bigs". Tina Schliessler photo]

The operator will give you the camera with the viewfinder open, focused to your particular eye with the lens aperture open wide and the tripod locks loose enough to permit your adjustment of the frame. If they don't, let them know that this is what you expect.

[Setting up a shot on *Max.* Kharen Hill photo]

Have a look. Get oriented. Reframe to taste. Lock the tripod. Give it back to the operator and say, *"Something like that."* The operator may tweak what you've done, but now they know what you're after.

The caution here is that whenever the director takes over the camera, *everybody watches*. If you don't improve on what the operator had initially, they're likely to think you're a bit of a poser.

Riding The Dolly

Same story with the dolly, but even more so. Because everyone can see that the dolly is fun to ride. If you ask to have a ride on the dolly, then offer up little by way of shot improvement, what was the point to this time you just wasted? A legitimate occasion for the director to ride on the dolly is when you have several story beats that need connecting and the planned dolly shot simply isn't doing the job.

The protocol is this: as soon as the camera is ready on the dolly, advise the camera/grip crew, *"I'd like to take a ride, please."* Ask your AD for stand-ins so you can see people in your shot. The operator will get off and you will get on. You'll ask the dolly grip to take you to "1st position." Once there, frame-up what you see as the shot opening, advising the stand-in/s where to be. Then say, *"That's 1st position."* The camera assistant will put marks down for the actor, the dolly grip will put down their mark, the operator will be watching the monitor, learning your intent. Then tell the dolly grip to start the move. Tell the stand-in, *"Action."* Work your way through to the 2nd position. Ask for everyone to stop. Advise this is 2nd position. And so on as you compose your shot down the line.

There's no point being overly fussy with precise framing or smooth operation. That's the operator's job. When you get to the end, thank the grip. Give it back to the operator, asking, *"Is that clear?"* They may have observations or suggestions. For example, they may ask if they can tuck an invisible zoom into the move to keep what you need in shot. That sort of thing.

Riding The Crane

Exact same deal with the crane except even more so. Because while the crane is a lot of fun to ride it's also an extremely complex tool. An inexperienced director can waste a lot of time fumbling around on one. Plus there are safety issues. If you're going to ride it, you'd better come up with some great ideas while you're up there. Many production reports go back to the PM/producer with a note like "*½ hr idle while dir played on crane…*."

The protocol: advise the AD and operator you'd like a ride. The operator will advise the crane grip. Many cranes have *counterweights* that need adjustment to your weight before you can get airborne. It's critical that you listen carefully and follow the grip's exact instructions when getting on or off. If you upset the delicate balance of the rig, *several thousand pounds of steel come crashing down onto the crew.* This also could look bad on the production report.

When the grip advises you to get on, do so. They'll often put a safety belt on you. Then put your eye to the camera and request they take you (and the stand in/s) to first position. If you're inexperienced or have issues with heights, don't take your eye away from the viewfinder. It can be alarming. Go through the exact same procedure you'd use on the dolly. Compose the shot. When it's time to get off, listen to and follow the grip's instructions to the letter.

Planes, Trains, and Automobiles

They're all camera-carrying vehicles. But the bigger they are, the more dangerous, expensive, and time-consuming. So it's even more important that you have communicated your vision during prep via conversation, storyboards, and an exact shot list on the day.

All of the above notwithstanding, you have the right and responsibility to utilize the tools in the toolbox to the best of your ability. Frequently the best way to do this is to take the camera and have a look around. The very fact that the director *isn't* a professional operator or pilot or driver is often what gives them a way of conceptualizing a shot that an expert would never think of. Riding the crane, a good director always spins around looking for other cool stuff. Any time the director puts their eye to the eyepiece, there's always the potential for coming up with something fresh and new.

Just be aware that a tremendous amount of time can be consumed getting in and out and on and off these devices. If your rationale is simply to "have a look-see," save the time. Leave it to the pros.

With respect to aerial shooting, riding in choppers is cool — at first. But they're dangerous and hard to use. This is a case where a clear shot list is vital. The camera operator in a helicopter is almost never your regular operator — it's a guy who comes with the rig. So you'll really need to be clear, on the ground, on exactly what story beats need to be expressed.

[With Dean Friss shooting green screen on ABC-TV's *Angel Flight Down*. Tina Schliessler photo]

When The Director Isn't The Boss

It's critical to note that while the director has a great deal of authority on set, when it comes to moving vehicles (and stunts and FX), there are other crew people whose authority supersedes the director's.

Say you're shooting from the specialized crew-carrying camera car. When the operator or grip advises the director to buckle in to a safety harness, this is not debatable. It's an *order* the director must follow. Otherwise the operator can and will refuse to move. Likewise, the director can't hop on or off to chat with an actor whenever the spirit moves them. There are various signals used for stopping, starting, and so on. Again, the grip, in concert with the AD, will dictate this.

In the case of aviation, particularly with helicopters, the director is under the authority of the pilot at all times. The pilot will tell you how and when to approach the craft, how and when to exit, and how to conduct yourself while on board. Even the director's artistic directions are subject to the overriding authority of the pilot. If a director requests something the pilot feels exceeds acceptable safety margins, the pilot can and will refuse the request.

Playing With The Toys

Movies frequently have cool toys in them. Planes, fast cars, bikes, whatever. So obviously that stuff is going to be found on a lot of movie sets. And frequently the transportation department will encourage the director to have some fun. Should you?

[With Colleen Rennison, Eva La Rue, and Jason Wiles on *Out of Nowhere*.
Tina Schliessler photo]

This can be iffy. I went for a ride in an unbelievably powerful Shelby Cobra on a show just for fun. And it was a lot of fun. The lead actor then asked if he could. He ended up in the ditch.

These toys are usually dangerous. That's what makes them fun. Say the director takes the Cobra out, hits a tree, breaks some bones. The entire production grinds to a very expensive halt. Frequently director insurance policies specify that dangerous behavior is not covered. A director who spends a lot of time playing on set creates the impression that they don't take the work very seriously. Try to imagine Woody Allen zipping around set on a Harley.

SECOND UNIT

If the director's authority is limited when shooting from dangerous craft, why bother even going? Why not let 2nd Unit worry about it? In fact, many directors do just that. But there are pitfalls here as well.

The 2nd Unit is a reduced crew with a separate director, DP, AD, the various crafts, and especially the stunt team. The 2nd Unit does not work with actors. Their job is to do the time-consuming, dangerous, often remote work that it makes little sense to have the 1st Unit shoot. On large action films, the 2nd Unit's schedule can be as long as that of the 1st Unit.

2nd Unit can be a contentious issue. Sometimes the 2nd Unit director is hired by the PM without consulting the director. They're often a stunt man, a camera operator, an AD. Someone whose primary skills do not lie in the area of storytelling. And even though the material they shoot may not conform to the director's overall vision of the show, it is sometimes edited in and released under the director's credit.

I was watching 2nd Unit dailies on a picture I was doing. I had provided the 2nd Unit director precise instructions for what was needed. Specifically, insert shots in an extremely realistic and panic-stricken gunfight. In dailies I was horrified to see a series of takes of a random gunman running toward camera, two guns out and blazing, Tarantino style. Multiple blood hits erupting from his chest. I asked the 2nd Unit director what exactly he was thinking. He told me he thought it looked cool....

Sometimes producers who wouldn't dream of letting a non-factory-trained mechanic work on their BMW will routinely let someone with no storytelling skills direct important sequences in their films and TV shows.

The Solution

There isn't one. So deal with it. Be polite and friendly to whomever it's expedient for them to assign to you to work with. Try to impress upon the 2nd Unit director what the story beats are. Make concise shot lists. Watch their dailies and correct them the second they start improvising. Of course the real solution is for producers to involve the director in the hiring of one of the many highly trained 2nd Unit directors that are always short of work. And of course that's what good producers try to do.

SCRIPT CHANGES ON SET

Partway through the afternoon everything's going great. And then suddenly we hit a wall.

We're in the middle of blocking a complex scene with a number of actors. There's a bunch of physical business, say cooking and eating. We've got entrances and exits. We're setting up a wonderful master that will eliminate the need for all the POV coverage a dinner scene normally requires. Suddenly an actor stops and says those fateful words: "*I'm sorry. My character wouldn't do this.*" And it all comes to a screeching halt.

What do you do?

1. First the director usually says something like, "*It's working fine for me.*" No sale.

2. Then the director will offer a cosmetic change: "*I see your point. Hmmm. How about if you came in through that door instead?*" Still no sale.

3. This is getting serious. Now the director starts damage control. "*OK, let's just finish blocking and we'll work on it somewhere else while the crew finishes lighting.*" To which the actor replies, "*What's the point of lighting me in places I don't even know why I'm going to?*" Damn. Welcome to one

of the director's worst nightmares. Set Screenwriting 101 in full view of the cast and crew.

The first thing to do is get the AD involved. They should call a short break and clear the set while we get it worked out. An audience for this kind of thing only increases the tension and hardens everyone's position.

And sometimes if we take the problem seriously enough to clear the set, the problem turns out to be less severe than imagined. A bit of discussion, a few subtle line changes, a shift in emphasis here and there, and the actor will realize that this is about as good as it's going to get. Problem solved.

This is a strong argument for working at being tight with the cast. I've had situations where I knew the actor was right. In one particular case I disagreed with the script element in question myself. I knew how to cut around it in post. And I just didn't have the time to deal with it. I just said, *"Look, you've got to trust me on this one. I know this is wrong. But make yourself do the best you can with it and I promise you I'll make it right in post."* We shot the scene, went on, I slashed the scene in post.

But it doesn't always go that way. Sometimes people get stubborn.

Occasionally it's because the actor has been angered by a specific thing. Maybe a costume is bothering them. Maybe their trailer is awful. Stuff I could have learned if I'd had a coffee with them when they came in this morning. Less often the actor is feeling insecure and argumentative just because they're psycho or bored, a pure mind game, the "script problem" is a figment of their imagination. Hollywood lore abounds with horror stories of psychotic episodes with actors who wouldn't come out of their trailer. Or refuse to say certain lines. Or otherwise terrorize productions, all out of sheer insanity.

I was visiting a set where a legendary Hollywood actress hated the producer so much she told the grip to erect a big black flag between her and the video monitors so she wouldn't have to see their faces. I spoke with her. She was charming, sensitive, and *very* angry. Know what she was ruining the show over? The producer had put her in a hotel way out of town and wouldn't give her a driver on the weekend. A few hundred dollars.

I've been lucky. I've worked with my share of allegedly "difficult" actors. But like Will Rogers, I've rarely met an actor I didn't end up liking. My experience is that actors *hate* to screenwrite on set. They want to do the scene and move on. But when something is wrong, *they know they're the ones who ultimately will have to wear it.* How many times have you heard someone say things like, "*Uma Thurman was so stupid in* Kill Bill. *Why didn't she just bring a gun?*"

People Rarely Argue Over A Scene That's Working

The most common reason actors hold up production over a script issue is, they're right. The scene makes no sense. The director complained about it in prep. But the writer/producers dug in their heels. The director said, "*How am I going to ask an actor to say and do these things? What's their motivation?*" The writer/producer's easy answer was, "*Um, money?*" Well, here we are. You figure the actor is motivated by money? Really? Should we offer them a few bucks to shut up and get back to work? It doesn't work that way. But to say the actor is right rarely means they know how to fix it. They just know it's broke. So how do we fix it and move on?

The AD will have a call put in to the producer to let them know there's trouble in paradise. The producer will often go through the condemned man's seven stages of denial before they begin a process of negotiation. How little change will the offending cast member settle for? The director in this case takes on the thankless role of a mediator running back and forth between the Palestinians and the Israelis. Finally a solution will be negotiated and accepted. Result: a considerable delay, an undermined director, an actor who's discovered a great new tool for next time, and a truncated scene. Lose/Lose.

There's Got To Be A Better Way

If the director has earned the producer's confidence, the way forward is much clearer. You take the cast aside and go through the scene beat by beat. Lay it out. It's often not that hard to pinpoint what's ruining a scene. It's actions or words or a combination of both. "*I wouldn't do or say that.*"

Actions are the less difficult of the two — do something else. But when it comes to the words, searching for pithy dialogue often slows the whole process to a crawl. Actor Michael Biehn (*Terminator, The Rock*) taught me an effective way to break this logjam. He calls it the "stick man" approach. Instead of trying to write good dialogue as you discuss scene fixing, just say "stick man."

So if you have actors playing a modern Scarlett and Rhett struggling over the realism of their dialogue, just ask the actor, "Well what is it you want to say to her?" Nine times out of ten your actor will say something like, "*After Scarlett tells me she really loves me and all that stuff I wanna look at her and say — 'stick man version' — Hey Babe, who gives a shit?*" Great. Now we very quickly create actual dialogue that gets this across — in character.

There's another type of problem. Many actors have a knack for zeroing in on that specific thing in the script that's forcing their character to do things their character wouldn't do. But what happens when that thing is something that *really needs to happen* for the story to go forward?

Say the script has an actor doing something inconsistent, but the story won't work without it. Solution: *try giving it to someone else in the scene.* Almost certainly there is another actor in the scene for whom this particular bit of behavior or dialogue would be much more in character. Let *them* do it. Result: a short delay, a cast that knows their director is a storyteller, an improved scene. Win/Win.

Earning the producer's trust and respect is critical. If the director has been cavalier toward script change in prep, or if they came in with poorly thought-out ideas, the writer/producer knows the director has little respect for their script. It's a prep note, but this is where the rubber meets the road.

It's never too late to earn the producer's trust. Get the producer on the phone and explain the problem. Suggest a conservative solution. But respectfully let the producer do their job. Sooner or later trust will grow.

Shooting Cut-able Stuff

Sometimes the director can try to get the actor to say and do what's in the script PLUS some other stuff the actor or director feels will make it work. But only if the other stuff is cut-able and takes very little time to shoot. I once had an antagonist who was convinced his motivation in a scene should be that in the backstory the leading lady had rejected his advances. I considered it a confusing idea. But we were tight for time. So I let him do it and he turned in a remarkable performance. When the producer asked me what the hell was going on, I said, a) the extra material is fully cut-able and b) that motivation really helped his performance come to life. The producer said, *"Good answer."*

[Dead Larry on *Heart of the Storm*. Mark Mervis photo]

Shoot it Both Ways

I did a sci-fi show where the lead character played by Ice-T was locked up in a virtual prison. His solitary confinement cell existed only in his mind. My intention was to shoot the inside of the cell from the prisoner's POV: cell walls, bars, rats, etc. But from the outside, from the other prisoner's

POV, he would just be sitting on a pedestal. No walls, no bars, nothing. The point would be made in juxtaposing the two points of view. It was a cool idea.

The trouble started when the art department asked me what color to paint the *outside* of the cell. I said don't bother. We'll never see it. The designer called the producer who called me. His position, "*Well how are the other prisoners going to know he's in solitary?*" Huh? I discussed it with him. I debated it, argued it. Finally, I strained our relationship by asking if we could shoot it both ways. We did. Problem solved. They kept my version but I don't recall anyone ever admitting they were wrong.

Sometimes that's the best you can do. But shooting like this wastes time and gives everyone clear proof that there's creative disunity among those steering the ship.

It's Just So Wrong

Sometimes a director is put into a position where they have to shoot something they know is totally wrong, Something they know is going to harm the project. There's a way to deal with this too.

Hit your mental Fast-Forward button. Visualize yourself in the editing room a few days/weeks/months from now. Visualize yourself and the editor tearing out your hair and trying to cut around this heinous mistake. Visualize the editor saying, "*If only you had shot a* ____." Now fill in that blank. What's in that blank? Here's a place your friendship with the script supervisor could pay off. Ask her to suggest something. Make a game out of it. Because there is always *something* you can shoot that will quietly save the scene.

Over My Dead Body

Sometimes in cases like this a director will feel so strongly they are right that they will do the unthinkable. They will simply shoot it the way they want and to hell with the consequences.

In James Clavell's heroic novel *Shogun*, the Blackthorne character claims that ignoring the will of your commander isn't treason *as long as you win*.

And of course that's the lure of treason on a film set. As the director you know that if you do what you've been told, the show could be ruined. Whereas if you take the law into your own hands, the show will be saved. Or so the thinking goes.

This is a no-brainer. When you're in a situation where you're considering on-set treason, ask yourself: If I do this will the show win an Oscar, an Emmy, or a Palme d'Or? *Will independent and very loud voices acknowledge the rightness of my choice such that my future employment is secure?*

Think about it. If this is an episode in the series *The Littlest Hobo*, the only meaningful review you're ever going to get is the next call from this producer or network. Think they're going to call the person who defied them? I'm not saying to just roll over. I'm saying to measure the cost/benefit and make an informed choice.

DIRECTING STARS

Directing stars is like directing actors only more so. On a star-driven project the star knows that they are the reason you're all here. And the reason *they* are here is to be great in a successful piece of work and thereby continue being a star. As long as they believe that their director is accomplishing that, all will likely be well. But the minute they feel that their director is compromising that goal, there will likely be conflict.

It's that simple. It's that complex.

The Shooting Stars

On the way up most directors meet stars who are on the way down. Sometimes spectacularly so. How does a director handle that? I suggest with gentleness and respect. If you are honest with yourself, you have to admit that regardless of this person's ability to do you any particular good, they have scaled a peak you haven't. And possibly never will. If your love for the entertainment business is genuine, that alone should command the respect due them.

When I meet a star, regardless of the current rating accorded them by the anonymous list makers and gossips at *TMZ* and on the *E-Tonight!* shows (like the IMDb "STARmeter" that has me up 38,304 today — whatever *that* means), I always try to find an honest way to say something like, "*It's a real honor to meet you. I'm excited to be working with you. I can't thank you enough for the pleasure I've had watching your work.*"

Stars, rising or falling, are people. Some you'll hit it off with. Others not. You'll do fine as long as you try to be straight, fight for your vision, listen, and learn.

Non Actors

Sometimes you'll find yourself working with non-actors for one reason or another. Sometimes the freshness they bring can really enhance the show. One thing to remember: these people often don't know our jargon or understand our methods. Be direct.

On my first feature we found a local hot-rodder in the small town we were working in who had a cinematic car and an interesting look. I wrote him into the background of the story. Everything he did played very well. Finally I decided to ask him to become a speaking character. The problem was we had no budget to pay anyone so I felt a little hesitant about asking. I took him aside and said something like, "*Um, Mike, ah… I wonder if maybe you might want to do a couple of lines with Pete and Tina.*" His instant answer: "*Heck no. I stay away from the powder.*" Be direct.

Death In The Afternoon

What everyone on the unit looks forward to as the afternoon wears on is that we'll work at a steady pace all day and finish five minutes before wrap. An early wrap, even if it's only five minutes early, can be a huge psychological boost. It doesn't always work out that way.

Real trouble rarely comes in the morning. It may but you generally aren't faced with the consequences until the afternoon. The clock begins to loom large. It's becoming clear that the time you spent rewriting that scene this morning is actually gone. And it's never coming back.

It's a terrible feeling. One moment you think you're making film history. Suddenly the AD looks at her watch and the matrix shifts. Whatever the reason there comes a time in many an afternoon when it gets real clear real fast: you're not going to finish your day at this pace. What do you do now?

Stuff You Can't Get Blamed For

On one picture I did, a lamp operator left a fixture too close to a sprinkler system head while we went for lunch. By the time we got back there was a foot of water covering the entire set. To a director, that's *force majeur*. The insurance covered the cost of cleaning and the overtime. It wasn't the director's fault.

How about if the dolly breaks down during a complicated shot and we lose two hours getting a replacement? Technically it's not the director's fault. But the shot could have been changed. It could have been shot on sticks or with the Steadicam. It wouldn't have had the aesthetic appeal the director was going for, perhaps. But while the delay isn't technically the director's fault, maybe not everyone is going to see it that way.

Inevitably, the director must face this question: Should I rush and risk spoiling my day's work? Or should I hold the course and plunge the unit into expensive overtime?

Playing Catch-Up

The first job is to perform the calculations. Based on how quickly the unit has worked in the past, it's easy to calculate how much work they're capable of. If the unit does three set-ups an hour, and there are three hours left in regulation, that's nine set-ups. If you need another twelve set-ups, your situation is pretty clear. Reduce your shot list, or go into overtime. It's like the NASA guys trying to get the Apollo 13 crew home with 30 amps and a role of duct tape.

Don't just stand there. First, do something fast. Cancel the complicated shot. Do a simple master to get as far as you can. While that's getting built, make a plan to simplify the remaining work.

The One-er. Short scenes can often be shot in a one-er. One shot with no coverage. If there's little dialogue and what there is works well, one-shot scenes can speed up the process considerably.

Two Position Blocking. As alluded to earlier, instead of blocking the master with everyone's face more or less open to camera, choose to have one or more of the cast plant themselves with their backs to camera. This accomplishes two things: a) the B camera gets an over-the-shoulder close-up simultaneously with the A cam master; and b) all we owe is one turnaround set-up to get the back to camera close-up/s. We just saved an entire setup. That puts us twenty minutes further ahead than we were a minute ago.

Block Shooting. Although unattractive, it can save a tremendous amount of time. I refer to the practice of shooting everything in the location that faces the same direction. One after another, regardless of how many scenes are involved. This saves the turning around to re-light time. But it's *ugly*.

The Steadicam. It's an article of faith that a director can shoot their way out of trouble with the Steadicam. The logic of this is, to hell with the look. We're in so much trouble we'd shoot it with Mom's handycam if we had to. The problem with scenes finished this way is that they look different. Different worse. It's better to realize we're in trouble before it gets this bad. But if one is down to the lemons of 30 minutes until dark, get creative. Mount up and make lemonade.

OVERTIME

Most shows go into overtime once in a while. Some less, some more. The best time to discuss O.T. is in prep during scheduling. If the schedule puts more on any one shooting day than the director feels they can do, they must let the producer/s know that an O.T. situation is likely on that day. This is key. Serve notice that you are concerned that the quality of the filmed material shot that day could be seriously compromised because of time pressure. So when the heat is on in the last few hours, the producer is less inclined to get pushy.

Why would a producer get pushy? Because O.T. costs money. A lot of money. It disrupts the schedule. Suddenly everyone's call time has to be pushed for the next day. And now you're running out of light for *tomorrow*. So the pressure goes up. Leaders are judged by their grace under fire.

This means overtime

CALL SHEET

		Date:	Thursday
Place	Latest Script Revision	Crew Call:	
.C. V7M 3G3	Double Yellow Pages	Shooting Call:	__
39/Fax(604)980-4159		Lunch Call:	
	ADD _ HRS TO ALL CALLS	Day:	16
		Sunrise:	0801
		Weather:	Cloudy
/ilkinson		Rain	

SET DESCRIPTION	Pgs	D/N	CAST	LO
sey's Apt - Bedroom	3/8	N1	1,2	River
take Love				500 l
sey Apt	1 6/8	N1	1,2	
and Madeline Relax				
ver	1 4/8	N3	1,2	
he and Casey pack and run				
B Unit				
of	2/8	N1	9,13,15	
l Guys Shooting				
/er	1 5/8	N3	9,13,15	
s Men Advance			Atmo A,B	
er	4/8	N3	9,13,15	
s Men Split up			Atmo A,B	
	1/8	N3		

[Typical call sheet detail]

The second you step into O.T., you're under fire.

The pressure comes at you from various places. Obviously there's the financial pressure coming at you from the line producer. There may also be pressure from the crew, who can sometimes make it pretty clear they are not happy about working late. An actor may need to catch a plane. You yourself may feel personal pressure from a previously made family commitment, a date, just plain weariness.

Fight The Pressure

Ignore it. Insulate yourself from it. Focus on the shots you need to create the scene. Tell the story.

It also doesn't hurt to acknowledge that these are unusual circumstances. That you are aware of the pressure. That you do not take it lightly. In O.T. I always ask the producer what increments we're working in. In some jurisdictions the unions give a producer very small increments of time. Sometimes 15-minute blocks. In other jurisdictions the units are half-hour or one-hour minimums. If there's an hour minimum, it makes no sense to rush to finish in half an hour. Likewise, if the increments are 15 minutes, a few minutes one way or the other can be important.

The Overtime Bottom Line

Based on how severe you perceive the crisis to be, you make a new plan. You pare your shot list down to the minimum number of shots you can tell the story with in keeping with the tone of the show. You present your plan. Then you stick to your guns.

Because there is one thing the working director has to remember about overtime. The line producer may say how much trouble the budget is in. They may promise they'll make it up to you. They may beg and plead. But if you rush to finish and turn in sub-standard work…

No one will thank you. You alone will take the blame.

Too Tired For Safety

My first major car chase. Two hours into O.T. We were pushing hard. Everyone was bone tired. The grips were racing to take the ancient beater Mercedes chase car down off the camera trailer where we'd been shooting dialogue and gunfire. They slapped the wheels back on the car, unchained it, and rolled it off the trailer. The operator, the stunt driver and I bailed in with a camera. We accelerated up to 50 MPH or so on our police-controlled, traffic-free, midnight riverside road. We shot some excellent high-speed over-the-hood driver POV. When we arrived back at the set, a grip took me quietly aside, white faced and shaking. He pointed at one of our wheels. Four of the five lug nuts — the nuts that hold the wheel on the car — were *missing*….

THE ABBY SINGER

There's a prolific AD who became known throughout the industry for a practice he was said to have engaged in frequently. As the story goes, towards wrap time, Abner "Abby" Singer would often call for just one more shot. The director would think of something else. Mr. Singer would then call for just one more shot. Amusing as this may be, the humor can fade late at night when everyone just wants to go home. You'd be amazed how fast the indecisive director can become an Ed Wood.

So what does it mean when the AD announces on set that this is the Abby Singer? It's the second to last shot of the day.

The Window Shot

As in, "*When do [win-dow] we get to go home?*" Seriously. When the director advises the AD that this is the last shot of the day, the AD announces to the crew that this is the window shot. This sets in motion a rush of off-set activity that various departments must do before they go home. But imagine how impressed the crew is going to be if their Window turns out to be an Abby. So....

That's a Wrap

That's it. Thank the actors. Shake hands with the keys. Off you go. One down, however many more to go.

[With R.H. Thomson under a large wind machine on *Max*. Tina Schliessler photo]

chapter ten

THE BIG PICTURE

MENTAL FATIGUE

It's 11 p.m. on a Friday of the sixth week of shooting. You're two hours into overtime. The cast and crew just want to go home. You tell your AD this is the window shot. A surge of relief washes over the unit. Out of the blue the producer shows up with some suggestions for three or four pick-up shots someone at the studio has asked for. Inserts, reaction shots, rib shots (the filmmaker digging the audience in the ribs and saying "*get it?*") And suddenly it all hits the fan. From some deep well a great blast of anger and frustration suddenly erupts. Your heart rate accelerates, your face reddens, your mouth opens to tell him to go to h….

Let's freeze time right there.

You're tired. He's tired. You're all tired. Tired people have shortened tempers. It's science. You've been averaging five hours of sleep per night for the past six weeks. The crew's been getting more, but they live harder too, so it evens out. This means that you are all much more likely to react in anger for reasons you would find non-angering when you're adequately rested.

Let's flash forward now. It's one year later. The picture came out. It did OK. You suspect that the producer has never quite forgiven you for getting angry that night over the shots he wanted. In any case, he hasn't hired you for any of his current shows. The phone is maddeningly silent. Your memory starts to do one of those shadowy transitions, back to a night just one year ago. There's the producer standing in front of you with a list of pick-up shots he wants. Your heart rate is accelerating. Your face is red. Your mouth drops open and you say, "*Why don't you just go to h…ave a cup of coffee while we shoot those for you.*"

My Mind Is On The Blink

Tired is the worst possible state to be in when making decisions that could impact your future. So don't. Tell yourself to breathe in and breathe out. Calm blue ocean. There will be plenty of time later to get angry if you still want to. The first casualty of weariness is judgment.

Is there anything a director can do about the mind-numbing weariness that comes with the job? Yes, there is. Anything that promotes rest is good. Get as much sleep as you can. Eat small nutritious meals. Don't eat a big lunch on set. Don't party too much on the weekends. Don't drink excessively. Laughter is good. So is yoga. Meditation works very well.

United We Stand

This is another case where building human relationships with your co-workers can make the difference between getting the day or going down in flames.

I've learned to recognize the signs in myself. When I begin to feel irritated I always stop and see if it's due to tiredness. If so, I'll tell the AD, the DP, the script supervisor, "*Hey, I'm getting tired, are you?*" Usually that degree of honesty provokes an honest answer. And it encourages us to ignore the petty irritations, pitch in, get something simple and beautiful, and go home.

The flat-out best method of driving away weariness-induced irritation: visualize yourself wearing a suit, working in an office….

THIS TOO SHALL END

When you're in the midst of a shoot it's hard to imagine not being in production. It's so all-consuming you rarely reflect that in a few days or weeks you're going to be sleeping in. But you will be. Unless you hop directly onto another show. Which is great from a career POV. Not quite so great from a personal POV.

The Note On The Fridge

Pick a big director from a few decades ago. A blockbuster type. Someone you haven't heard of for a while. Want to know where they are now?

Many are retired and doubtless living well. But the odds are that a fair number of them are in expensive houses on the beach in Malibu with a nice car, expensive golf clubs, a handful of friends, no kids, no grandkids, no partner, pretty much alone with their golden statuettes. Sound like someone you want to be?

One of the best things about being a working director is the time off. Because shows usually don't happen back to back. Because the pay is usually high enough to eke out a careful existence without working non-stop there's often a lot of time to spend building a life. My personal experience has been that when I direct a movie it's largely forgotten in a few years. But family keeps getting better and better over a lifetime.

[Author with sons Pablo and Fabio on *Max*. Kharen Hill Photo]

Features and episodics are the worst homewreckers. And it's not just the director's problem. The entire cast and crew suffers. We spend all of our waking hours for months on end bonding with a group of attractive friends, digging deep in emotional terrain to create something beautiful. How relevant are our partners or our kids going to seem? How long do you think they'll take this?

But....

You have to keep working. Say no too many times, or even once to the right project, and your career can nosedive.

The reason I'm talking about this here is that your current job is often where your next job comes from. A working director gets more work. People see your name on one thing and they think, "*Hmmm, they must be good. They're directing.*" Don't wait too long to trade on this. As mentioned earlier, unless your current show wins an Oscar or an Emmy, you are probably more hirable *before* the show wraps than after it plays.

WHY ISN'T YOUR AGENT CALLING?

Your agent needs to be beating the bushes for work now. It's important to talk to your agent when you're shooting. Most agents would deny that when you're working they feel less pressure to keep you serviced. But it's a fact of life. I don't mean they ignore you when you're working. They just feel slightly less pressure to sell you than some other director they rep who has promise but is about to go stale. And slightly more or less pressure is often the difference between getting the next job or not.

Changing Lanes

But what if you're directing a syndicated series, an action drama. Let's say something in space. Say you feel you belong in features. Here's where the quicksand is: if you stay too long anywhere, *that's* where you get stuck. How much feature heat does a director with 15 episodes of *The Office* generate? Think a studio exec is going to say, "*We need a good, solid, reliable director for our $200-million space drama. Hey, let's get that director with 15 episodes of* The Office." Uh huh. Know who's got a real chance? The guy with one Miley Cyrus music video to his credit or a cool commercial for Audi.

You can't stay too long in a place you don't want to be. If features is where you think you should be, then do one episode. Maybe a couple. Don't buy that Porsche. Save the money to carry you through the time off you're going to take to direct a no-budget show with Sundance potential. A good filmmaker friend of mine refers to this concept as "*self-unemployment.*"

These are some of the hardest choices the working director will face. The conflict between career, money, lifestyle and family has no easy answers. Every job you take or pass on is a crap shoot. And we all like to believe we're on a path, not a treadmill.

THE WRAP

Finally the last week of shooting approaches. The last day. Then the last hour. It suddenly becomes clear that this is all going to end. The end of shooting is a lot like the end of a transatlantic flight. Suddenly a tremor goes through the plane. The cabin attendants bustle about, collecting headsets. Everyone starts preparing for re-entry to life on the ground.

On a film set it's ushered in by a wave of cell phones ringing. Suddenly everyone is on the phone in their spare moments. Hustling the next job. Snatches of overheard conversations about how many weeks, such and such a location, so and so a star, this studio, that network. Keys offer work to their people. Or not. Actors call agents. Have they heard so and so is shooting such and such?

For the director this flurry of activity can feel a bit like treason. We're still working on this show, right? And then there's the card exchanging, number giving, promises of "we'll get together." All told, it's kind of like the last day of camp. "*We'll always be friends, call me as soon as you get home....*" And like the promises kids make on that last day at camp, the promises movie people make to stay in contact are really hard to keep.

You know how guilty everyone on the set feels about ignoring their families while they work on this show? Well they're all about to go on to other shows where they will again feel guilty about ignoring their families. Plus now they'll feel guilty about ignoring all the friends they made on this show. Set relationships fade. Just like summer camp friends. But there's always next summer. One of the best things about remaining in this business for a while is that if you stick around long enough you'll get to be with these people again and again.

One practical note is to keep the cast and crew lists. You often forget the names but you'll always remember there was a great sound person on such and such a show.

Celebrate

"That's a wrap." The last shot of any picture is usually an emotional moment. Whether the show was a good experience or a bad one, the last shot means a lot. It means you've gotten through it.

For the director it's especially thought-provoking. Wrapping means saying goodbye to a group of people you've grown very close to. It means saying goodbye to the make-believe world you've all been creating and living in. And it means saying goodbye to the creative power a director has. It means going home to whatever is waiting there. It means unthinkingly saying to your partner, *"Could I get a coffee?"* And your partner (if they have any sense) responding, *"What, do I look like? Craft Services?"*

THE WRAP PARTY

Go. You owe it to the unit, to the picture, to yourself. Besides, wrap parties are a lot of fun. They're a way of getting closure with these people. They're like this giant decompression chamber. The director walks in the door as "the director" and walks out a human being again.

I'm assuming you're a popular director. If you aren't, consider giving the wrap party a pass. There was a director who was very unpopular with the crew on a show in the midwest one winter. A grip warned the director not to come to the wrap party. He did anyway. The crew buried him up to his neck in a snow bank and left him there for a good long while. This was the same director who at an earlier mid-summer shoot offended the crew to such an extent that when he and his extra/date opened his rental car door at wrap, he was knocked down by a gusher of rotting fish. I think they were maybe trying to tell him something about his management style.

People do surprising things at wrap parties. Mostly good things. They can relax now. They're not auditioning for the job. It's over. Suddenly the 2nd AD is up on the stage singing with the band… and he's *really* good! The most unlikely people can dance. And it's always startling to see a team of people you've never seen out of work clothing suddenly appear in dresses and make-up (especially the teamsters).

For the director, the wrap party is a weird mix of feelings. Your entire focus for weeks, months on end, has been getting the shot, the scene, the performance. Now that's all done. Whatever the show is going to be, the major part of that has ceased being hypothetical. It really is carved in stone now. You wonder, everyone wonders, what it's going to be like. You know a lot more about the movie than anyone else. But you don't really know the one thing everybody wants to know: is it going to be any good?

And at the wrap party there's that unavoidable question, "*What are you doing next?*" Like it's some kind of measure of your ultimate worth if you're going on to bigger and better, or more of the same, or unemployment. For the director it's especially hard because most crew people work a lot more than most directors. So frequently they'll all have jobs lined up and you've got post-production on this. And then God knows what.

At the end of the day, every movie wraps, it plays, the reviews end up wrapping fish, the trophies tarnish, the money's gone. What's going to be left? Here's the sort of thing I value:

Dear Charles,

I couldn't have asked for a better director to work with on my first TV movie. Thank you for having confidence in me, for your support, and your friendship. Working on *The Ruby Silver* will always be a wonderful memory! ★

Sincerely Jonathan Jackson

[With Jonathan Jackson on *The Legend of the Ruby Silver*. Tina Schliessler photo]

Celebrate the achievement. Wish everyone well. Let it go. Everyone else is winging their way home or on to the next job. But you're headed for the cutting room.

chapter eleven

Post-Production

The Post Process

The post-production process functions differently on different shows, but there are enough common practices from which to generalize. The editor assembles and edits the filmed material as it comes in. Ultimately they produce what is called the "editor's cut." Once shooting ends the director sits with the editor producing a "director's cut." Then unless the director has final cut rights in their contract (very rare), the producer screens the cut. Often they accept it as is. Sometimes they will ask for (or simply make) changes. The picture is finally "locked." The sound is edited. The Visual FX (if any) are created. The music is composed and recorded. The soundtrack is created and mixed. The colors are corrected. The titles are put on and it's released.

For the director, post is a radical change of gears. You've just come from a noisy set where you had a hundred people coming at you from every direction with a million things all at once. Here in the editing room, it's quiet. One on one. Just you and the editor. Post-production is a lot more technical than production because mechanization is much more prevalent in post. All of the machines have names, specific functions, and are capable of an almost infinite variety of creative effects.

The problem for the director in post is in knowing what you want, knowing what you're likely to get, knowing how and when to ask for it. The process is flexible, but it's inherently linear. In other words, the process likes to build B on A, C on B, and so forth down the line. So although the bad color timing on an otherwise useable shot may irritate the director, if you make the editor stop picture cutting to fiddle with color balance, you waste valuable time.

And time is, again, the director's arch enemy. There's a post schedule. There's an "air date" or a "release date." There's rarely sufficient time to explore all of the possibilities in the footage you've shot. So the director's key to post becomes understanding the process in order to direct it as effectively as the shooting.

THE CUTTING ROOM

"The Cutting Room" has a magical sound. And magic does happen there. But the physical reality is anything but. It's usually a small, windowless room with a desktop computer, a few drives, two monitors, some near-field speakers, a client screen. There are two or three chairs, maybe a couple of call sheets pinned to the wall. Glamorous it isn't.

Here's how the production chain works: you shoot footage on set during production. If it's film, it goes to the lab. They process the footage, transfer it into the digital medium. Then the data goes to the edit facility, where an assistant loads the dailies into the computer hard drive. Somewhere along the line copies of these "dailies" are made for the producer/s, director, DP, etc. The editing systems vary and change, but what they all do is store the shots in folders organized by scene. The editor then begins to assemble those shots into edited scenes and the edited scenes into a completed show.

The computer-based editing systems can perform a wide variety of visual and audio effects. The software is able to fade, dissolve, speed ramp, do fast and slow motion, color correct, add titles, modify the sound for volume and equalization. It can also perform interesting visual effects. Photoshop-like stuff. But the editor is usually far too busy to play with that. They leave everything but the actual picture cutting to specialists. The editor concentrates on cutting the story.

What Exactly Is An Editor?

Forget the images Hollywood gives us of a humble clerk huddled over a Moviola, obediently gluing the director's shots together and nodding admiringly at every insight that drops from the director's lips. Think instead of Perry White. You know — the hard-bitten, tough-as-nails newspaper editor that Clark Kent and Lois Lane work for. Perry shouts and raves. He takes Lois Lane's promising but disorganized story copy and *edits it*. Sometimes he even *re-writes* it into something he feels people will understand and respond to. A good film editor doesn't usually rave or smoke cigars, but the newspaper analogy holds. A film editor doesn't simply join shots together. *They create a living, breathing story out of the elements they're given.* Sometimes with help from the director. Sometimes not. The editor is a storyteller. On the same level with the writer and the DP.

During the entire time the director was shooting the picture, the editor was cutting the material as it came in. They may also cut problem scenes together for the director from time to time. Plus checking things for the producer. Editors typically spend 12–16 hours a day at the keyboard. They generally don't get paid overtime. Editors experience eye strain, carpal tunnel syndrome, posture and weight problems. It's not particularly healthy work.

Editors work at different speeds on different types of shows. In episodic TV and on TV movies it is not uncommon for the editor to have a pretty good cut ready a few days after wrap. On features there is generally a lot more time to explore the possibilities, so the pace is slower.

In any event, the director usually calls the editor a few days prior to wrapping the show and sets up a time to come in and start work on the director's cut. The editor usually wants some time to get their cut so they have something presentable to show the director. They will usually send a copy of this assembly to the director a day or two prior to their arrival so the director can make notes.

The Director in the Cutting Room

When the director arrives for work in the cutting room, the editor will usually screen the entire show for the director. They'll talk, agree on a plan of action, then get to work. The editor sits at the keyboard touching the controls. The director sits behind the editor. Watching, commenting, *directing*.

Every editor has their own procedure. It's worth paying very close attention to get a sense of how each individual works. Editors tend to cut for
meaning first. Because if the scene doesn't tell the story, there's no story.
So as the meaning gradually becomes clear over the course of the editing
process, the editor tends to focus more and more on the *feel*.

One very common cutting technique that can confuse inexperienced
directors is the "radio cut" style many editors use to cut a dialogue scene
that has a lot of overlaps. They'll first cut the audio together to form a
rational-sounding conversation. Then they'll put the right pictures with
it. Until the moment the procedure is completed it all looks like gibberish
to the uninformed.

A director who understands the process will know enough to wait for
the editor to finish before commenting. But sometimes it's hard to know
if they're finished. They're sitting in front of you hunched over their keyboard, tapping away. The picture starts to run. Is that it? Am I supposed
to say something now?

When I worked as an editor I remember directors saying, "*Let's go to
close-up a beat earlier.*" I would make the cut. I'd preview it once and see
it needed a few frames trimmed. But the director would go, "*Nah, doesn't
work. Let's try….*" So what am I as an editor supposed to do? Agree with
my director and move on? Even though I know the right thing to do is
adjust the cut? Or should I stop and argue?

What Editors Hate

There's a behavior directors sometimes exhibit in the cutting room that
drives most editors crazy. The director will be watching a shot then leap
up and point at (even touch!) the screen and shout, "*Cut there!*"

Um, editors know how to cut from a wide shot to a close-up. It's what
they do. Editors don't need schooling from a director on how to make a
dissolve or an overlap. Appropriate comments are things like, "That feels
a little slow" or "Try cutting the coverage with more dialogue overlaps"
or "I'd like to stay in the master quite a bit longer." An editor will take
a request like that and implement it — without you telling them which
buttons to hit.

Which raises another sore point for editors. Don't touch the machine. Keep your fingers off the buttons. Some editors are comfortable with a director taking a scene away and cutting it themselves. If they have the extra equipment and don't feel offended or threatened by this, it's often great for a director to work this way. But feel it out carefully before you ask. You're going to be in this room with this person for a while.

EDITING FIXES

Say there are problems in the area of meaning. If a particular story beat is not coming across clearly, the director has a variety of tools. Re-shooting is best. But few shows have the budget to bring actors and crews back. A much less expensive insert shot will often help, if there's budget for any 2nd Unit or insert unit shooting during post. Always ask the editor to insert a "scene missing" card if a pick-up shot is planned. Otherwise you could grow so used to looking at it without the card that you'll gradually stop being aware of how badly you need the additional shot. Plus a (by now) cash-strapped producer just might say, "*Works fine for me. We don't need it.*"

An off-camera line of dialogue can often work wonders to get a story beat across. And if you're bringing cast back later for ADR anyway, it's a "free" solution. But during editing it's important that you sell the idea of adding a line. Again, there are two ways of doing this: 1) tell everybody; and 2) show everybody by recording the line. The latter method tends to work best.

Tell the editor you want to record some off-camera lines. They'll ask their assistant to have a mic standing by. You can read the line yourself (or ask a handy member of the opposite sex if appropriate). Put some effort into it. Get into character. Mimic the voice you need. It's fun. It works.

Script Changes in Post

The editor will sometimes take one look at a scene and say, "*This doesn't work,*" then cut it the way you argued in prep to have it written. It's remarkable how pragmatic everyone gets about script changes in post. Often when the director asks for script changes during prep it's called "*artistic differences.*" When an editor arbitrarily reworks large pieces of unclear material it's called "*saving the picture.*"

Much of the work in editing revolves around removing redundant stuff. Audiences are smart. If you beat them over the head with it they lose interest fast. The director's role in post-production story editing usually begins with the words "*what if….*" And it's usually about what if we cut from this line to that one and throw out all the slow stuff in between.

The House Of Cards

Editors in the days of film used to get very defensive over their cut. In a way they had to. They were cutting actual film. If a director wanted to try it a thousand ways the film strip itself would turn into an "accordion." It would click and flip going through the gate of the Moviola. They'd have to order re-prints. It got expensive and very time-consuming. Frank Irvine, the wonderful old-school editor of *The Grey Fox*, used to say "*It's a house of cards. I won't change a frame.*" (This from a guy who took a wannabe director's first and only two-hour feature, cut it down to 24 minutes, and said something to the effect of, "*The rest is shit.*" He got his way too.)

[Assistant Will Waring with editor Frank Irvine on *My Kind of Town*. Charles Wilkinson photo]

Now that editing is "non-linear" digital, there's no limit to the number of cuts and versions an editor can make. But some editors still buy into the "house of cards" thing. Sometimes they're right. Sometimes they're being lazy. But as a director you have a right to see the material cut together as you intended. The editor has the obligation to show you. If it doesn't work, you'll see that.

It's In Your Contract And It Isn't

Director's Guild contracts all have language setting forth the director's rights during editing. And each individual director signs a deal memo that specifies how many weeks they are expected to work in post. There's also language that limits the director's rights. What it boils down to is this: make the picture work great within the time you have. That's all a working director can do. Regardless of all the careful thought you've put into the prep and all the sweat you've put into the shooting, the day you deliver your cut, the producer can cut in dancing girls if they want. This is one of the biggest reasons directors aspire to the ultimate control that comes with top status. It's just so heart-wrenching to see someone strangling your baby.

This is yet another example of how important it is to develop a good working relationship with the team. In this case the producer and the editor. They want the show to be good and people are hesitant to argue with their friends. But at a certain point the director has to trust the process. Your director's cut gets sent out to all the execs who have approval at the studio/network. If the producer takes over and really ruins the show, some execs may remember your cut.

And the reality is that most of the producers you work with (like most actors and crew) will be talented, committed individuals.

Temp Music

One great tool the director has for making their cut work is temporary music. Ralph Rosenblum, in his book *When The Shooting Stops... The Cutting Begins*, talks at length of how his knowledge of music enhanced his abilities as an editor. It's the same with a director.

The editor sometimes just doesn't have time to put good temp music into their cut. A director with a knowledge of music will have been thinking about and gathering temp music for this particular show since their first reading of the script.

A great place to look for temp music is on soundtracks from existing films. Many modern films release soundtrack CDs complete with underscoring, action scenes, love themes, everything. These make wonderful dinner music to play at home and when the director needs a track that says "modern dysfunctional youth joy riding through the slums," they'll reach into their collection for Stewart Copeland's amazing track from Francis Coppola's *Rumble Fish*.

DIRECTING MUSIC

There are two basic kinds of film music. When Tom Cruise sings along with Tom Petty's "Free Fallin'" in *Jerry Maguire*, that's what most people think of when you say film music. But that's only a small part of what film music is. The main part is called the *score*: the underscoring, the themes, the scary cues, the action cues. The "*da duh, da duh, da duh*" cue from *Jaws*. That's scoring.

High-budget shows hire well-known composers to create the score and frequently spend more on music than the average indy film's entire budget. Some high-budget teen-oriented shows feature numerous pop tunes as well.

Smaller-budget shows simply can't afford popular songs. Many indy shows have no place for pop songs. Try to imagine *Hard Candy* with a Justin Bieber single in it… But virtually all shows have some form of scoring. And for that you need a composer.

Music is an enormously powerful tool in the director's box. Music is second only to performance and camera for expressing emotion and creating mood. The director should always be on the lookout for musical ideas during shooting. Does the story's teenage kid have a rock band, however bad? Record them. Is the story a modern street drama set in Little Italy? How about blending mandolins with modern electrics? Is there a factory that figures prominently in your story? Are there rhythmic sounds the machines make? Ask the producer to have the sound mixer spend an hour recording the machines. A composer can make anything into music. Chains rattling on pipes can be a beautiful sound when taken out of context.

Choosing The Composer

In many cases on long-form productions the producer will invite the director to have input into choosing the composer. The producer and director will ask a number of composers whose work they know, composers who are available and can work at that budget level. You'll send them a script and invite them to audition. They play samples. They talk about what they hear for style, instrumentation, etc. Ultimately the composer who seems to have the most promising approach to the show is hired. The director works with them and a score is produced.

As director you should always keep in mind that you can go to a composer with a problem. Say the attraction between the two leads is not instantly obvious, but it needs to be. A talented composer can create the illusion that two people on opposite sides of the room are falling in love. Same thing with action scenes that need help. How scary would the *Psycho* shower scene be if instead of using Bernard Herrmann's terrifying score, Hitchcock had gone with the Bee Gees? When a composer works with the director as part of the storytelling team amazing things can happen.

Not Choosing The Composer

But often the working director has no input on who scores the show. Sometimes the producer has a relationship with a composer who can deliver adequate music on time and on budget. To the director it's less than ideal to have a composer whose number one goal is simply to get the producer's next show.

But there are ways of working within a shotgun marriage like this. If the composer is working for the producer and the producer has great musical taste, no problem. If the producer has less than great taste, look at it from the composer's POV. All musicians love music. They don't get paid enough to do it for the money. So if they're working for a producer who says, *"Just put some sweet stuff here and some scary stuff there...."* how engaged will the composer be? Any composer worth anything would much rather work for/with people who appreciate the process and push hard for excellence. And keep in mind that the composer can't be sure you're not the next top director. They want to work with you.

What Composers Hate

Composers tend to hate temp music. Directors put in these wonderful temp cues: rich, fully orchestrated pieces from *Black Swan* which everyone loves. Then the composer has to try to reproduce that with 5% of the music budget Clint Mansell had for that film. And suddenly everyone thinks the composer is lame.

Obviously a director should use temp music of a magnitude that the show can afford. If there's only $20,000 in the entire music budget, don't use temp from *War Horse*. There are lots of musical styles that aren't expensive. The most common and least interesting is the synth score. Lower-budget producers often use the synth score as an inexpensive substitute for orchestration. But live jazz groups playing PD or original material aren't necessarily expensive. Neither is piano or string quartet.

For songs there are always emerging groups that need a movie credit. They'll give sync rights to their songs for between little and nothing. And your show gets a hip, alternative feel.

Time Pressure — Again

It's a rule of thumb that the sooner the composer can give you something to listen to, the more likely you'll get something that works. The problem for the composer is *picture changes*.

If you had all the time in the world, the composer would wait until the picture was completely edited before starting the music. That way, when the girl takes the boy's hand, the composer can play a little flourish. The cue plays on, girl kisses boy, and there's a crescendo. And it's all in perfect sync. This kind of work takes time. But if the composer scores this scene and then the scene is re-cut the composer has to go back and edit or re-compose so everything fits again. Music editing is way more complex that picture editing.

DIRECTING THE SOUND MIX

The sound mix creates a sound track for your film that has clear and understandable dialogue, exciting sound effects, stirring music. All balanced perfectly. It also has the power to create and maintain the mood.

And if you thought picture editing was complex, wait until you sit in a large mixing studio. Typically it has a mixing console that stretches 20–30 feet long. On it, under it, beside it, and behind it are an array of high-tech components that make a 747 cockpit look like a pocket calculator.

[Mixing console at dbc Sound. Otis photo]

What Is A Mix?

This is a complex topic, but the director needs to acquire a certain amount of technical understanding of the mix in order to direct it effectively. Mix studios charge anywhere from a few hundred to a few thousand dollars an hour. The sound mix on a long-form can take anywhere from two weeks to two months. So it's obvious the director can't simply sit there and say, "*I don't like that sound, change it.*"

Simply, a sound mix is where everything an audience needs to hear in a movie is blended together in such a way to express meaning and mood. Typically there is a lead mixer with two mixers working under him. The lead mixer usually has responsibility for mixing all the dialogue. The other two deal with music and sound effects.

They sit at the mixing console, also called the "board" and manipulate the faders up and down to make sounds louder and quieter. They twist dials to add or subtract reverb, EQ, and various other types of effects. And they occasionally connect other "outboard" pieces of gear to filter out unwanted noise.

A Million Tracks

Why do the mixers have all those individual faders? Each fader represents one track of audio. To grossly oversimplify, say all of a certain actor's dialogue for the wide shots is on faders number 1 and 2. Their dialogue for medium shots is on faders 3 and 4. The close-ups are faders 5 and 6. In this way the mixer can balance the levels, the EQ, the reverb in such a way as to maintain the illusion that the scene happened within real time. Instead of what it really was — shot over the course of a long day with airplanes flying over one minute and not the next, heavy traffic during rush hour, and so on.

Add to this several tracks for any ADR that might have been recorded for the particular actor. Then multiply this times the number of actors in any given scene. That's why so many faders. And that's just for dialogue. Add to that as many as fifty sound effects tracks, twenty or more music tracks. It adds up.

The Director Preps For The Mix

During the later stages of picture editing, the sound editing team assembles and starts their work. The dialogue editor will assess the location recorded production track, check out alternate takes, make a list of ADR they think is required.

The sound effects (SFX) editor will do the same with the sound effects. They generate lists of what can be sourced from FX collections, what needs to be recorded in the field, and what the Foley team can handle.

And there will be a music-spotting screening with the composer. In this screening, decisions will be made about where music is needed and what it needs to accomplish.

Obviously, much of the prep work is of a routine technical nature and there's little need for director input. In fact, if the director never talks to any of the sound editors and doesn't bother going to the mix, the editors and mixers are more than capable of making the show sound perfectly adequate. It's when the director wishes for something unusual that conversation with these people is needed.

Say the director has strong feelings and desires about specific sound effects. Now is the time to let the head SFX editor know. If the sounds aren't recorded and placed on tracks for the mixer, they won't be in the show. And just as you avoided giving dumb directions to the picture editor, you really need to avoid wasting the sound editor's time with comments like, *"OK, when the bad guy shoots — his gun should make a really loud bang…."*

These people are good. They've done this a million times before. A good rule is: if you want a particular element to sound like other top shows in the genre, relax. That's what the sound people will give you. But if you want something unusual, you have to tell them.

[With Peter Svab cutting *Heart of the Storm* in L.A. Charles Wilkinson photo]

THE PRE-MIX

Once the sound editors have finished editing all of their various production dialogue, ADR, Foley, Sound FX, Ambiance and so on, they hand it over (generally in a digital format on one or more hard drives) to the mixing team. By this point it may be that the picture has been color timed and corrected. It may be that the visual effects have been finished and edited in. Sometimes even the titles and credits are done. So the sound mixers will be mixing to an otherwise completed film. The significance of this will become clear in a moment.

The mixing team needs to do a tremendous amount of purely routine work before the really creative part of the mix can happen. This is called the pre-mix. And the director and producers rarely attend all of this. Why not?

Take the dialogue, for example. All the dialogue for any given scene must be adjusted for volume, EQ, and especially background noise such that if you were to play the dialogue alone without any other added sounds it would sound entirely natural. In other words, although the background noise levels and mic placement may have been radically different between the master shot and the close-ups (where typically the mic can be placed closer, thus reducing background noise), each individual and often different sounding shot must be adjusted, filtered, noise reduced, turned up or down, until the entire scene sounds as smooth, clean, and seamless as the budget can afford.

In general the pre-mix sees the mixing team taking the often hundreds of tracks and pre-mixing them down into a manageable number of tracks. So that later in the mix when the director says, *"The dialogue in this scene is a little too quiet"* the mixer can simply raise the overall level of the dialogue without having to adjust every single track.

Virtually all film mixing boards are computerized and automated. So when the effects mixer slowly raises the volume of a particular sound effect over the course of a scene, the computer "memorizes" it. Every subsequent time the movie reaches that part, the actual fader on the mixing console will raise. *All by itself.*

If a director has the time it can be very worthwhile to drop in to the pre-mix and spend an hour or two each day. It helps to develop a working relationship with the mixing team and it familiarizes the director with the problems the mixers are facing. For example, let's say several scenes have borderline dialogue, say the background noise is quite high. If the director happens to be there when these scenes are being pre-mixed, it will become clear that the best one can hope for is to make that particular dialogue *adequate*. If a director isn't aware of this and they walk into the main mix and hear that dialogue, they'll likely waste hours having the mixers demonstrate why this dialogue can't sound fantastic.

The Mix Begins

The director is offered a chair at a desk above and behind the mixing console and team. In attendance are probably the picture editor, possibly the sound editor/s, the composer, the producer. The lead mixer usually offers to play back the entire picture. Just to give a sense of where they are and how far they need to go.

I mentioned earlier that the mixers are often mixing to a pretty much complete picture. Color timed, titles, everything. When they press "play" the picture fades up, the music begins, and….

You watch your movie for the first time!

This is the very first time this film has played with proper color, titles, music, effects, and clean dialogue. The impact on a director is often extraordinary.

From the moment you first read the script, this movie has existed in your imagination. One by one each component came into being. First the shooting, then the editing, then music, sound, visual effects, titles. As long as one element remained unfinished, the film has always remained partially imaginary. Now it's real. This is the show. Everything is there. Adjustments will be made. There will be shifts in emphasis. But if you or anyone in the production team has been deluding themselves about what it is you're making, now is the moment you absolutely cannot avoid confronting the reality of what you have actually made.

Sometimes it's a stunning surprise, a moment of real triumph. Sometimes not. Regardless of what your reaction is you're not being paid to watch the show. You're being paid to make it better. Don't let your reaction blind you to the many subtle things you can do to improve it.

THE MIX

So now you've seen/heard it. You have a sense of what the show is. A sense of what it needs. You may have made specific notes about changes you'd like. The most common mix notes are usually music notes. Notes regarding placement of music and relative loudness. It's not uncommon for a piece of music to conflict badly with the dialogue and sound effects. We'll get to that. But first things first.

The mixing team could use some encouragement, "*Nice work gentlemen, you really smoothed out the dialogue, etc.*" The lead mixer's position is a difficult one. They require a high degree of artistic and technical skill. They also possess diplomatic skills so finely honed that I sometimes think a good lead mixer could resolve the Middle East conflict in an afternoon. To say that tempers can flare in the mixing studio is an understatement. It's time to get to work.

The mixer presses "play." The projector flickers to life, and away we go. The team rolls ahead for anywhere between ten seconds and five minutes. Then they stop and go back to where one of them (or you) had a problem and re-start from that point. In this way they gradually work their way through the show. It's important you remember that the three mixers are not permanently blending their work together. The music can be totally wrong and yet the dialogue and effects mixers are happily working away achieving lasting perfection. Remember, the computer learns. It doesn't forget.

You hear something you're not sure of. Your mouth drops open to comment, to bring the team to a halt. Wait. The mixers prefer that you let things go forward for a while to see if it's something they've noticed. Usually it is and they catch it on another pass. If not, speak up. It's very unlikely the team will not have noticed something obviously wrong.

But where they may miss things is where sounds are supposed to be happening off-screen that have an impact on the on-screen action. Say the sounds of the gallows construction crew outside should be having an impact on the prisoners in their cells. The mixers will often need input on how much of an impact.

A tip: Use the *numbers*. There are time code numbers at the bottom of the screen. They usually measure elapsed time. Each reel starts at the successive hour. Reel 3 time code addresses begin at 3:00:00:00. So the second you notice something that sounds wrong you want to jot the number down on the pad in front of you. Then when they stop, an appropriate way to raise the issue with the mixers is to say, "*The hammering at 5:05 needs to be louder.*" They'll tap those numbers onto the pad and you're instantly back there. Conversely, amateurs identify themselves in a mix with comments like, "*The hammering back there before Jesse smiles needs to be louder.*"

If the director has a radical note, now is exactly the right time to express it. The mixers will work away doing what they consider to be normal sounding work unless they're told differently. As the director you potentially have enormous power in the mix. Your range of possibilities stretches from dead silence to deafening noise and everything in between. For example, sometimes a director will turn the dialogue down to nothing in a scene. They'll let the music play or the wind blow. It can have an amazing effect.

Likewise, a director can request a sound that isn't there. Say you suddenly realize that what your family dinner conversation scene needs is to remove the dialogue and replace it with the angry squabbling of a flock of penguins. Ask for it. Chances are the mixers have online access to extensive sound effects collections. If not, they'll ask the SFX editor to find one and fly it in. It normally takes only a few moments to deal with such a request.

Music Mixing

Composers hate directors messing around with their music. But sometimes it's necessary. Once I was mixing a long chase scene. The music was pounding rock. After a time it started to grate. I asked the mixer what the track layout for the music was. He told me the guitars, bass, horns, and drums were all on separate tracks. I said, "*Great, pull everything out except the drums at 11:21, let the drums carry us to 11:37, then slam everything back in.*" He tried it. It created a welcome respite in the action. Maybe the horn by itself will sound great. And how about drums and bass? Play with it.

Sometimes a music cue will sound completely wrong. It will fight with the dialogue or the FX. Or it will have the wrong tone. It's important to flag these cues right away. Let the composer know (if they're around) and they can start hunting for a solution. Sometimes the composer can remix the cue and bring it back. Other times they can create an entirely new cue. Most often they will suggest "lifting" a cue from earlier or later in the show. Something like, "*There was a great sting of low, ominous underscore in the title overture. Could we just lift that one note?*"

Hide That Flaw

Here's something weird. Most human brains only process one thing at a time. That's the principle magicians live by. Every magic trick takes place under the shadow of a diversion, a *misdirection*. That technique works at least as well in film. Say there's a moment in an actor's performance you hate. Say their eyes accidentally crossed the lens at one point. Tell the sound mixer to place a dog bark or a car start or something a frame or two just prior to the offending moment. It doesn't need to be loud. It's amazing how the offending moment simply *disappears*.

Turn It Up

Loudness is relative and there are physical limits to how loud movie sound can be. If you have a very quiet movie, a moderate sound will seem loud. If you have a show with wall to wall gun battles, at a certain point nothing is going to seem loud. What will happen in a mix session with a director or producer who doesn't understand this is that they'll keep telling the mixer to make the music or the effects louder. Which the mixer will do. He'll run the levels right up into the red. Then along comes a scene with a tremendous explosion. The mixer will be told to make that *really* loud. He's already at max. Where's he going to go? The answer is that he has to go back and undo all your requests to turn it up. So that when real volume is called for there'll be some room left.

A tip? Keep your eyes on the meters. They're big, right under the screen. If you see that the needles are spending most of their time near the top, know this: the theatre projectionist and the audience at home will simply turn your show down for you.

Fighting In The Mix

Directors rarely fight with the mix team. The mix team rarely fights with each other. But put two or more people in the room who all share some measure of creative power and the potential for conflict can loom large. One of my favorite producers ever, the venerable Allen Epstein (who was incidentally somewhat hard of hearing) once got so angry in a sound mix that he actually threw a chair across the room — a big upholstered swivel chair, not a little folding job.

As director, by this point in the show you're getting tired of babysitting and consensus building. You're tired of manipulating everyone to stop fighting long enough to do good work. But you have to hang on for just a bit longer. The director needs to exercise all their artistic, technical and persuasive abilities in the mixing studio.

The sound mix is the last place the director can make real improvements in the picture. After this, it's someone else's turn.

[With producers Jim Green, Mark Bacino, and Allen Epstein on vacation.
  Greg McDougall photo]

chapter twelve

IT'S OVER

F ade to black. Credits roll. Lights come up. Shake hands with the mixers and the sound editors. Hug the picture editor. Exchange compliments with the composer and the producer/s. Walk through the door out onto the street and it hits you. It's over. For the top established director the end of the sound mix is the beginning of a whole new phase. Promotion, festivals, interviews, articles. But for the working director this is often the end of the line.

We frequently have between little and no role in what happens after the sound mix. Most shows are not entered in festivals of any kind. Most directors won't be invited to do *Leno*. Most directors never even make the cover of their own guild newsletter.

It feels *weird*. After so much activity. So many calls. So many questions. And now, nothing. But there are a number of things the working director can and should do after the mix.

Get Copies

There is language in every guild director agreement regarding the director's copy. This is something you leaned on your agent about during contract negotiations, remember? What you need here is a copy of the show in a semi-permanent digital format. Formats change so fast now, and there's this huge rush to hard drive and flash drive based media. The question you need to ask is – are these media durable? At point of writing, the only archival medium is BluRay. It's so easy for shows to fade away. You worked hard. Preserve your work.

Thank You Notes

During post-production it's a good idea to select one of the best production stills you can find from the show. It's a simple matter to Photoshop the image into a cool souvenir postcard. You can send this out to the entire cast and crew thanking them for their contribution and advising them that the show is finally finished. It reminds everyone that you valued their work and it keeps people thinking about the show.

Do a slight revision of the card, changing the wording to make it simply an announcement that you've completed a new show. Then send it around to everyone who is in a position to hire you.

Send one out to each of the trade publications. They're always hungry for news of this kind. If they print it people will read your name in a positive context. If you live in a smaller community or even a distinct neighborhood of a large city there are almost always small local papers. They often welcome copy about the arts in the community.

THANK THE PEOPLE WHO BRUNG YOU

Send the above postcards to the network/studio/distributors as well. It's been a while since you wrapped. A while since you met face to face. They have other projects they're thinking about directors for. They should be considering you. Which they will the second that postcard hits their desk.

Stay in touch with whoever in the organization has current release date info. Prepare alternate wording for your postcard that you can send around for release/broadcast date to contacts, cast, crew, and friends.

PRODUCER CLOSURE

Take the producer who hired you to lunch. Ask them point blank if they're happy with the show. If they're going to recommend you. If they'd hire you again. If there were simple misunderstandings maybe it can be fixed. Remember what the producer I spoke of earlier said:

Everyone who is not your friend is your enemy.

Bad word of mouth can destroy a career. It can build and grow without any real basis in fact. It needs to be dealt with. If you hear or sense that someone is slagging you, talk to them. Usually the person you're concerned about is the producer who hired you. Hence this lunch.

Find out if they have been or are planning to bad-mouth you. Ask them straight out. Ask why. Make an effort to see it from their POV. If the show turned out awful and it's obviously your fault there's not much you can do. But that's usually not the case. Nine times out of ten if a producer is angry with a director it's because they feel the director didn't show them the proper respect. They feel the director exceeded their authority. They changed dialogue or adjusted story or went into overtime too often. That sort of thing.

I've known producers to post-lunch re-hire directors they pre-lunch wouldn't have hired to clean their septic tank. It's important to recognize how much history you two have together. How much less likely you will be to fight in the future now that you know each other's signals.

I directed an action show for producer Bill Vince (*Capote, The Imaginarium of Dr. Parnassus*). Although the show itself turned out quite well I had difficulty dealing with what I saw as Bill's frequent, clumsy missteps into the creative process. To Bill's credit he felt bad about it and made overtures to reconcile after the picture was done, but I couldn't. I was still pretty raw over it. Now he's gone. Bill was a good man. He deserved better.

You'll Always Work in This Town Again

Once in a while a show goes badly. Sometimes lasting enemies are made. When a working director experiences this and then goes through one of the slow spots that happen periodically it's tempting to think that a few too many bridges have been burned.

If everybody who has been warned that they'd never work in this town again actually didn't still work here, the town would be empty. Most people who bad-mouth are not respected. What kind of a person goes around saying nasty things behind other people's backs? Everyone has *enemies.* I seriously know people who are critical of the Dalai Lama. The trick is not to dwell on it. Keep working.

Directing Your Inner Writer

Some working directors spend off-time developing their own screenplays. Industry majors sometimes laugh about this. They say it's like an airline captain who secretly wants to be a cabin attendant. But directors write screenplays because they are storytellers. They write screenplays because it's one of only a few proven ways a working director is ever going to get material that could propel them to the next level. But there are risks. Writing takes months. Months of not chasing directing. If the script doesn't get made the director has now slipped way back in the pack.

I think some people are born with an extra writing gene. Their work is so brilliant. It seems so effortless. The rest of us have to work very hard to acquire even the most basic skills. Screenwriting is enormously complex. But with some time and effort it's possible to learn how to recognize a good script when you see one. It's possible to learn how to critique a script. To make a bad one less bad and a good one better. There are excellent books on the subject. My personal favorite is Robert McKee's *Story*. If you spend a few months studying McKee's book you may not emerge as a brilliant screenwriter. But what you will definitely acquire is a greatly enhanced ability to recognize what's good and to *fix* what isn't.

Shameless Self-Promotion Time

It's obvious you need to update your reel and resume and get it to your agent immediately. While you're at it, talk to your agent. What are you up for? Why not? What can you do? Who can you meet?

Show business operates on buzz. Most people never see most shows but *everyone* feels the buzz. So with the limited resources of a working director on a show you're no longer officially working on, get busy and create some buzz.

Festivals. The show you just finished is almost certainly eligible for a number of film festivals. There are festivals dedicated to infomercials even. There will definitely be venues for yours. You don't even need to win. Just get accepted. Get *short listed*. If you get rejected from enough festivals even *that* becomes an item: ("*See the film no festival dared to show…*") Festival activity looks great on your resume and many producers will happily let you submit the film. Do ask first, though.

TAKE A MOMENT

Whether you throw a huge party or hike alone up a mountain, this is a time and place you need to pause and pat yourself on the head. *You directed a motion picture.* That is truly an achievement to be proud of. Know this: Your family is proud of you. Your friends and acquaintances are proud of you. You have just done something an awful lot of people would give just about anything to do. Win, lose, or draw, you've touched the hem of the garment. Like Tolkien's Bilbo Baggins, you've been there and back again.

Take a moment to reflect on the working director's good fortune. As hard as it is to believe, people are actually paying us to do the most interesting, the most fulfilling, the most absolutely cool job in the world. See the picture below? The smiles are real.

Cheers to you for the success you've had. Do something beautiful with the amazing ride in front of you. Good luck!

[With a little help from my friends on Disney's *Out of Nowhere*. Chris Large photo]

ABOUT THE AUTHOR

C HARLES WILKINSON is a working director with extensive credits in film and television. He lives and works with his wife and extended family on a North Pacific coastal fjord near Vancouver.

Visit charleswilkinson.com

[On Haida Gwaii, British Columbia. Tina Schliessler photo]

THE MYTH OF MWP

In a dark time, a light bringer came along, leading the curious and the frustrated to clarity and empowerment. It took the well-guarded secrets out of the hands of the few and made them available to all. It spread a spirit of openness and creative freedom, and built a storehouse of knowledge dedicated to the betterment of the arts.

The essence of the Michael Wiese Productions (MWP) is empowering people who have the burning desire to express themselves creatively. We help them realize their dreams by putting the tools in their hands. We demystify the sometimes secretive worlds of screenwriting, directing, acting, producing, film financing, and other media crafts.

By doing so, we hope to bring forth a realization of 'conscious media' which we define as being positively charged, emphasizing hope and affirming positive values like trust, cooperation, self-empowerment, freedom, and love. Grounded in the deep roots of myth, it aims to be healing both for those who make the art and those who encounter it. It hopes to be transformative for people, opening doors to new possibilities and pulling back veils to reveal hidden worlds.

MWP has built a storehouse of knowledge unequaled in the world, for no other publisher has so many titles on the media arts. Please visit www.mwp.com where you will find many free resources and a 25% discount on our books. Sign up and become part of the wider creative community!

Onward and upward,

Michael Wiese
Publisher/Filmmaker